MARK GRUENWALD

FREDERICK LUIS ALDAMA, SERIES EDITOR

MARK GRUENWALD

PAUL V. ALLEN

UNIVERSITY PRESS OF MISSISSIPPI / JACKSON

The University Press of Mississippi is the scholarly publishing agency of
the Mississippi Institutions of Higher Learning: Alcorn State University,
Delta State University, Jackson State University, Mississippi State University,
Mississippi University for Women, Mississippi Valley State University,
University of Mississippi, and University of Southern Mississippi.

www.upress.state.ms.us

Title page portrait by Antony Hare

The University Press of Mississippi is a member
of the Association of University Presses.

Copyright © 2026 by University Press of Mississippi
All rights reserved
Manufactured in the United States of America

∞

Publisher: University Press of Mississippi, Jackson, USA
Authorised GPSR Safety Representative: Easy Access System Europe -
Mustamäe tee 50, 10621 Tallinn, Estonia, gpsr.requests@easproject.com

Library of Congress Cataloging-in-Publication Data

Names: Allen, Paul V. author
Title: Mark Gruenwald / Paul V. Allen.
Other titles: Biographix
Description: Jackson : University Press of Mississippi, 2026. | Series:
Biographix | Includes bibliographical references and index.
Identifiers: LCCN 2025045080 (print) | LCCN 2025045081 (ebook) | ISBN
9781496861436 hardback | ISBN 9781496861443 trade paperback | ISBN
9781496861450 epub | ISBN 9781496861481 epub | ISBN 9781496861467 pdf |
ISBN 9781496861474 pdf
Subjects: LCSH: Gruenwald, Mark | Marvel Comics Group | Cartoonists—United
States—Biography—Comic books, strips, etc. | Editors—United
States—Biography | Comic books, strips, etc.—United States—Biography
| Superheroes—Comic books, strips, etc.
Classification: LCC PN6727.G7655 Z54 2026 (print) | LCC PN6727.G7655
(ebook)
LC record available at https://lccn.loc.gov/2025045080
LC ebook record available at https://lccn.loc.gov/2025045081

British Library Cataloging-in-Publication Data available

> Comics have never been just a hobby to me, nor even just my favorite form of entertainment. Comics relate to everything I do and have done. They are the single unifying strand in the ordered confusion of my life.
> —Mark Gruenwald, 1976

CONTENTS

Prologue... 3

CHAPTER 1.
Origin (1953–1971) 5

CHAPTER 2.
College Years (1972–1976) 15

CHAPTER 3.
Into the Omniverse (1976–1978) 27

CHAPTER 4.
Writer and Artist (1978–1984) 38

CHAPTER 5.
Mark the Editor (1982–1987) 49

CHAPTER 6.
The Official Handbook of the Marvel Universe (1983–1993) 60

CHAPTER 7.
Squadron Supreme (1985–1989) 68

CHAPTER 8.
D.P.7 and the New Universe (1986–1989) 77

CHAPTER 9.
Captain America (1985–1995) 87

CHAPTER 10.
Mark the Executive Editor (1987–1993)................... 95

CHAPTER 11.
Quasar (1989–1994) 103

CHAPTER 12.
Death and Afterdeath (1995–present) 113

Epilogue 128

Acknowledgments 131

Notes 133

References 143

Index 151

MARK GRUENWALD

PROLOGUE

Circa 1974, twenty-one-year-old Mark Gruenwald took it upon himself to paint a triptych depicting scenes from the story of Jesus Christ, a figure he considered the "archetypical superhero." To dramatize the crucifixion properly, Mark decided he would need a photo reference.

As was his usual method on his myriad creative endeavors, Mark recruited help. He worked with his father, Myron, to build a twelve-foot cross rigged with rope loops for the hands and a pedestal to stand on, as well as a ladder for climbing up. He called on his friend Roy "Chuck" Hoglund to drive him to an open space between a landfill and in-progress housing development that had huge mounds of dirt and garbage that could stand in for Calvary. Mark himself, with his lean frame and long hair and beard, would be the model for Jesus.

Mark and Roy set everything up, and Mark stripped down to a white loincloth, likely fashioned for him by his mother, Norma. He climbed up on the cross and directed Roy as he snapped photos. As they worked, cars began to line up on the nearby thoroughfare, and an audience of gawkers formed. Soon, Mark and Roy heard sirens approaching.

The cadre of police—including a highway patrolman and the sheriff—delivered a stern warning about disturbing the peace, and insisted Mark and Roy go home. Rather than feel chastised, Mark was thrilled by the whole experience. To him, creating a spectacle was an integral part of creating.

After he finished painting, Mark sold the triptych to a local church for $250. If the church officials noticed Jesus's resemblance to the artist, they didn't let on.

CHAPTER 1

Origin (1953–1971)

> Comic books affected me a lot when I was young, and impressed a number of good values upon me—improving my vocabulary and exciting my imagination.
> —Mark Gruenwald, 1979

Mark Gruenwald's relentless creative impulse was part of a family tradition. Myron and Norma Gruenwald were outgoing, artistic, and restlessly busy. Mark's dad was a singer, actor, a teacher, and an amateur historian. He served on the board of the public library, was president of Northeast Wisconsin Education Association, and self-published several books on Pomeranian history and genealogy. His mother was also a singer and an actor, as well as a crafter and a beautician. When Myron began to suffer from the effects of Lyme and heart diseases, Norma started her own chapter of Mainstay, a support group for spouses of the chronically ill.

The couple met through Norma's cousin when Myron was home on leave from the Army, where he was serving as a sergeant during the Korean War. They fell in love instantly, despite a four-year age difference and dissimilar backgrounds. He had spent his youth in the city of Oshkosh, Wisconsin, and had just one brother; she grew up on a farm thirty miles away in New London, and was the seventh of fourteen children. Norma's parents didn't approve of the romance, partly because she was only seventeen, so Myron and Norma decided to elope. In November 1951 they traveled to Wartburg College in Waverly, Iowa, and tied the knot. The couple settled in Oshkosh, and on June 18, 1953, they welcomed a son, Mark Eugene. Sixteen months later, daughter Gayle rounded out the family.

When Mark and Gayle were growing up, Oshkosh was the picture of a midcentury midsized midwest US city: supper clubs and drive-in diners, neighborhood markets and drug stores, a thriving downtown with a variety of shops and movie theaters. It was home to Wisconsin State College Oshkosh, a former teacher-training college that was on its way to becoming the third largest university in the state. The city was steadily expanding in the postwar boom. In 1960, when Mark was seven years old, the city had a population of about 45,000 people.

Mark's childhood was also what one might picture as the midcentury, middle-class ideal: He rode his bike around the neighborhood with his friends until the sun went down; in the winter they went ice-skating on Lake Winnebago; his paternal grandparents—Eddie and Lu—lived just up the street; he was a Boy Scout, with his father as troop leader. When he was born, Mark's family lived in a duplex on Sawyer Street, located on the west side of Oshkosh, but in 1956 they moved into a two-story white house located at 605 Sawyer.

When Mark was little, his mom worked at the Mueller Potter drugstore on Oshkosh Avenue, which had a rack of comics in the front window. When visiting his mother, Mark had free reign with the merchandise. Though he initially gravitated toward Harvey Comics (*Casper the Friendly Ghost*, *Wendy the Good Little Witch*, and so on), the 1952–1958 *Superman* TV show led Mark to purchase his first superhero comic: *Superman* #127 (February 1959), in which Superman battles Titano the Super Ape. A few months later he expanded out with *Flash* #108 (September 1959).

Myron had been a comic reader as a youth, witnessing the 1938 debut of Superman firsthand. Mark, in turn, was the perfect age to experience the Silver Age revival of superheroes. When Mark discovered the Justice League of America (JLA) in *The Brave and the Bold* #29 (May 1960)—he'd somehow missed their debut in

The Gruenwald family dressed up for Easter, 1957. Courtesy of Gayle Coughanour.

#28)—he became obsessed. He'd later say that the JLA's adventures "grabbed ahold of my adolescent imagination like nothing else." The first sixty-five JLA stories would form the foundation of Mark's superhero ideal, and for the rest of his life he could recite the titles and plots chronologically, and would chase the feeling those stories inspired in him.

So strong was Mark's love of the JLA that he couldn't bear the wait between new issues. "I decided to start drawing my own stories to while away the time in between," he recalled. "Every Sunday afternoon my dad, mom, and sis would go to my grandparents' house for dinner and I'd spend all my non-eating time working on my ongoing superhero opus, making up the story as I went along, drawing with ballpoint pen and Crayolas on ruled tablet pages." When he filled up a tablet, he'd start a new one. In all, he filled twelve tablets with his own JLA adventures.

Neighborhood kids gather to admire Mark in his Superman costume, 1963. Courtesy of Gayle Coughanour.

But reading about superheroes and creating his own superhero comics still wasn't enough. Mark wanted to *be* a superhero. Norma was an excellent seamstress, and she taught Mark to sew. Together they made costumes, Superman for Mark, Wonder Woman for Gayle. They marched in the annual Ohio Street Children's Day Parade wearing these, pulling along a wagon adorned with some of Mark's favorite comic books, though he worried the whole time they might get damaged.

Around this same time, Mark started a JLA club, encouraging friends around the neighborhood to each take on the persona of a member of the team, costume and all. Keith Boushele was Batman, Lee Ziebell was Aquaman, Jeff Paffenroth was the Flash, and Randy Domer was Green Lantern. Their Mount Justice was located in the loft above the Gruenwald family garage. Myron had built the space, which was only accessible by ladder, so Mark could have a clubhouse. At meetings, the JLA club would show off, trade, and talk about their comics. They designed their own flag, wrote an anthem, and engaged in mock battles egged on by Myron, playing "Roboster, the Robot Master."

In 1961, *Fantastic Four* #1 debuted. Mark didn't jump on the bandwagon because Mueller Potter didn't initially carry the newly established Marvel Comics. But on a family trip to Racine, he came across *Fantastic Four* #8. A few months later, distribution in Oshkosh improved, and Mark was able to start buying *Fantastic Four* regularly, along with all of the books that followed soon after and formed the foundation of the Marvel Universe as we know it. Mark bought *Amazing Spider-Man* #1, *Avengers* #1, and *X-Men* #1 as they came out. Marvel didn't displace Mark's love of the JLA, or his preference for DC, but they had a "crude sense of danger and excitement" he found appealing.

Mark decided to start a Fantastic Four Fan Club with a completely different membership from the JLA club. The group made their own T-shirts, and, as club secretary, Mark wrote in to the *Fantastic Four* letters page. His letter saw print in *Fantastic Four* #20 (November 1963), ironically after the club had already disbanded; Mark had found he preferred the Avengers. However, the letter served as Mark's introduction into the larger comic book fan community, as he subsequently received letters from other fans around the country.

As Mark made his way through fourth and fifth grade, his friends lost their interest in comics. By sixth grade the JLA Club was no more, and Mark was the only boy his age who still bought and read comics. So when his mother gently suggested that maybe a young man going into junior high should give up collecting comic books, Mark agreed. This happened to coincide with money being tight for the family, due to Myron leaving his job as an engineer at Rockwell Standard to attend the University of Wisconsin–Oshkosh. So Mark didn't just stop collecting, he decided to sell his collection. That summer he set up a card table normally reserved for Gayle's Kool-Aid stand, and put up a sign that read "Comics:

5 cents." Within a few days most of his books were gone. He gifted his Superman costume to a younger boy who lived next door.

Mark put his energy toward other pursuits. He was a Boy Scout in Troop 1 (he earned four Eagle Scout badges before losing motivation to continue). The family joined First Congregational Church on Algoma Boulevard in downtown Oshkosh, and became heavily involved, with Myron serving as a lay minister, Norma teaching Sunday school, and both of them singing in the choir. Myron and Norma passed their love of music to both Mark and Gayle, and Mark got an acoustic guitar he taught himself to play. Reading comics had piqued Mark's interest in astronomy, mythology, and science fiction. He and Myron loved to watch *The Twilight Zone* and *The Outer Limits* together.

It was a time of change for the Gruenwald family. In 1966 Myron finished college and began teaching sixth grade at Smith School near downtown. The next year, the Gruenwalds purchased a brand-new construction west of Highway 41. The Westhaven development—advertised to potential residents as a way to get away from the "hustle and bustle of the city"—represented a 10 percent increase in the size of Oshkosh. The Gruenwalds would be one of the first ten families to live there. Besides being brand new, the house at 1260 Westhaven was much bigger than the house on Sawyer, with a full basement (Mark painted the floor in an interlocking orange, green, and blue puzzle design) and four bedrooms. Myron and Norma allowed Mark to have two rooms; one for a bedroom and the other a studio and workshop.

The small number of initial families in the Westhaven development resulted in a tight-knit community. Mark became best friends with a boy his age, J. Mark Madison, who lived across the street. Mark and Gayle rode the bus to school for the first time, and met lots of new people that way as well. Mark told his father that it felt like his life began after they moved to Westhaven.

Mark began his eighth-grade year in the fall of 1967 at the newly opened Perry Tipler Junior High School. He served as editor-in-chief of the school newspaper, *Tipler's Tiger Tale*. For the first issue,

Mark penned an editorial called "Establishment of Tradition." He grandly compared the opening of the school to the founding of the United States, encouraged his fellow students to get involved, and wrote, "the way we do things this year may very well set a pattern for years to come. We should be concerned enough to set our standards high, so later we will be able to look back and be proud of our contributions."

He followed his own advice. In addition to editing and writing for the paper, Mark played the role of minister-turned-serial-killer Reverend Harry Powell in an English class production of *The Night of the Hunter* (the role performed by Robert Mitchum in the 1955 film), and won a pin from the Oshkosh chapter of the Daughters of the American Revolution for "superior work in the American History course." He also continued to write and draw his own comics, including the adventures of a superhero team he called The Psychic Syndicate and an eighty-page story called "Night of the Sleeper."

He had started reading comic books again. This was surreptitious at first, but by the end of seventh grade Mark was back to collecting as if he'd never stopped. If he worried a bit that resuming the habit was an indication of immaturity, he got over it quickly. He would even bring the latest comics to school to read during homeroom.

✏ ✏ ✏

Oshkosh High School was where Mark really blossomed creatively and socially. Mark made fast friends with the other kids in his accelerated classes, and found a steady girlfriend in classmate Jane Archer. According to his friend Roy Hoglund, the Mark of this time looked "like a guy who would be reading poetry in a coffee shop," with thick wire-rimmed glasses, long wavy dark brown hair, and a mostly black wardrobe.

Appropriately, he took over the school magazine, *Spectrum*, and remade it into an alternative newspaper that included stories, poetry, opinion pieces on issues of the day, artwork, as well as "spoofs, scoffs and put-ons." Mark did a bit of everything on

Spectrum, aided by Jane, J. Mark Madison, and several other friends. Mark and his team mass-produced the publication with a mimeograph and distributed them in homerooms each Friday to subscribers and anyone else who was interested.

Seemingly tireless, Mark also continued to write and draw his own comics. His major project during this time was a 235-page "visual novel" called *Concept*. The story concerned a trio of amnesic super-powered characters. Even as a teenager, Mark wanted to innovate. He later recalled, "I decided to make the whole book an attempt to defy some of the time-honored traditions of the superhero comic while still remaining in the genre." The success Mark felt in translating his vision onto the page helped him realize that making comics for a living was a goal that was within his reach. Even so, he didn't take art classes in high school, having decided—wrongly, he'd later admit—that it wouldn't help him get better at making comics. He'd based this on his experiences in art classes in junior high, where he'd butted heads with his teacher over his tendency to turn every single assignment into something involving superheroes.

After his relationship with Jane Archer ended, Mark's attention turned toward Holly Lindsay, with whom he shared several accelerated classes. Holly was involved in music and theater, and served as captain of the cheerleading squad. Though she found Mark to be funny, smart, and creative, she wasn't too sure about dating at first. But eventually they became a couple.

In some ways he was an ideal boyfriend—leaving Holly a funny note in her locker every day, and inviting her to be part of his myriad creative projects, including working on *Spectrum*—but in others he was a bit clueless. During a picnic in the Wisconsin Dells, which Holly had envisioned as a romantic getaway, Mark took the occasion to instruct her on the complete history of the Fantastic Four. Though Holly had little interest in comic books, she drove him each week to a newsstand shop on Oregon Street and 9th Avenue to buy his comics, and patiently took dictation on a fourteen-page letter to Marvel editor and writer Stan Lee.

During Mark's junior and senior years he ranged outward even more. He became a deacon at church, ministering in junior church services. He was chosen (along with Gene Wright) as a Badger Boys State representative for model government. He acted in original plays, "The Will" (an *Oshkosh Northwestern* article singled out Mark as a "great ad-libber") and "The Featherless Bi-Ped."

The project that encapsulated Mark's creative range and ambition in high school was a musical called *Icarus*. During Mark's senior year, English teacher Gladys Veidemanis arranged a school media fair, and encouraged her students to think outside the box to create a multimedia project to present. Inspired by *Jesus Christ Superstar* and The Who's *Tommy*, Mark decided to create a rock opera version of the Greek myth.

Mark recruited friends to help bring *Icarus* to life. Gene Wright helped him write the story and lyrics. He enlisted Roy "Chuck" Hoglund and Charlie Haasl, who had a garage band called Dust, to help him write the music. J. Mark Madison contributed, too. The songs' styles showcased the various rock and folk Mark loved: the Doors, the Moody Blues, Cat Stevens, and Simon and Garfunkel. He cast Jerry Backus in the lead, with Gene playing Daedalus and Holly as Andrea, Icarus's girlfriend, whom Mark invented for his version of the story.

When it came time to record the production's six songs on four-track reel-to-reel, he found players on the drums, flute, and organ. To make it a true multimedia project, Mark illustrated forty scenes from the story in ink and watercolor, shot them on 35-millimeter film, and then converted them into slides to project in concert with the songs. In addition to presenting *Icarus* at the media fair, Mark also showed it at the Latin Club's annual Roman banquet, at the annual conference for the National Association for Humanities Education, and even put on a live performance in his backyard.

Mark graduated in the spring of 1971 with high honors, and was one of four students selected by the senior class to speak at commencement on the topic of "Society and Change." Mark's grades, awards, intelligence, and ambition made him a prime candidate for

Mark's senior photo, 1971. Courtesy of Gayle Coughanour.

any of the nation's best universities, but he surprised his friends by deciding to stay at home and attend University of Wisconsin–Oshkosh. While not a bad school, the university wasn't held in high regard among Mark's friend group; they all called it "U-W-Zero." They were headed for private liberal arts and Ivy League schools, and eventually for careers as professors, lawyers, and doctors.

But Mark already knew he wasn't going to be any of those things. He was going to make comics.

CHAPTER 2

College Years (1972–1976)

> Augmento: "Do you have any idea how hard it is to read your comic strip?"
> Mark Gruenwald: "You mean—it's supposed to be easy? This is college Augie!"
> —Mark Gruenwald, 1975

In many ways Mark's college life was a continuation of his high school life. He continued to live at home, be involved at First Congregational, and work part-time at a music store called The Record Shop. He kept reading and making comics, and he kept refining *Icarus* with Roy Hoglund and Charlie Haasl. Even his relationship with Holly Lindsay stayed steady, at least until October of freshman year when he visited her in St. Paul, Minnesota, where she was enrolled at Macalester College. There, she told him she thought they were on different paths and should split up. He replied, "No. If I come to Macalester can we stay together?" But Holly remained firm, and Mark returned home heartbroken.

And though he would have a couple more steady girlfriends in college, most of Mark's energy went toward creative pursuits instead of romantic ones. In keeping with his ambition to work in comics, Mark had decided he would major in art. As in junior high, he fought vehemently against his instructors' attempts to direct his focus away from superhero illustration. Mark would later express regret over his stubbornness. "By studying the masters and not-so-masters of comic art and disregarding other influences, I was guaranteeing that I would never be anything more than watered-down versions of the artists I admired . . . I should have drawn from life, made my own observations about how to translate the world into scribbles on paper, rather than aping someone else's observations." Eventually UW-O's art department gave in and let Mark create his own independent study course in comic art and storytelling. Among the projects he did during this time were a 263-page sequel to *Concept* called *Threshold*, a spinoff he titled *Galactic Trinity*, a Justice Society story, and a Wonder Woman tale. In all, Mark would write and illustrate over 600 pages of comics as a teenager and young adult.

He also engaged in several multidisciplinary extracurriculars. He finalized an expanded version of *Icarus* (which he presented publicly in March 1972) and worked on a follow-up rock opera called *The Sisterhood* (which concerned a futuristic society where women are the dominant gender). He also joined a modern dance troupe, which started with Roy and Mark enrolling in a dance class to earn physical education credit. Their initial motivation was the fact that they'd be surrounded by women, but the duo found they enjoyed the class. When instructor Cecelia Brown suggested they join Terpsichore, the dance club, they agreed.

Terpsichore became yet another outlet for Mark's creativity and leadership. He loved creating choreography, and he even took over leading the group's warm-ups. Spurred by Mark's drive and enthusiasm, the group worked up about six numbers. They began to tour locally to perform for other dance classes and clubs. In an article about Terpsichore in the UW-O newspaper, the *Advance-Titan*, Mark said, "Dance allows you to become less inhibited about your body and helps you to relate to other people . . . it's an instrument of self-expression through movement."

His senior year, Mark created a ten-part radio play based on *Concept*. Inspired by radio serials, Adam Strange comics, *The Twilight Zone*, and the Firesign Theater comedy troupe, *Concept Radio Theatre* was a mix of science fiction and satire, with tongue-in-cheek dialogue. It also explored some big themes, such as everlasting life and the role of religion in government. Mark recruited a large number of friends, college faculty, and even his father to act in the drama. Charlie Haasl used a Moog synthesizer and an Echoplex to create sound effects for the characters' superpowers (including mind-fogging, matter-bending, and teleportation), as well as time machines and flying saucers. The series aired in the spring of 1975 on the University of Wisconsin–Oshkosh radio station. Mark, with typical bravado, told the *Advance-Titan* that *Concept Radio Theatre* was "the *War and Peace* of science fiction radio."

"He always had half a dozen things going on at the same time," Roy recalls. Once, as they were leaving an art class together, Roy witnessed Mark going down the steps two at a time, and asked why he was doing that. Mark replied, "If I get down in half the time, then I can use that extra time for something else."

Despite his explorations of other creative mediums, Mark's greatest impact at the UW-O would be in the realm of comics. *Augmento* was a superhero spoof created by sophomore Bill Bukowski that debuted in the *Advance-Titan* in 1973. Bill did twelve strips that spring featuring the bespectacled, long-haired character with a treble-clef on his torso. Despite the premise, the feature had less in common with mainstream superhero comics than they did the underground comix that had come to prominence in the late 1960s due to artists such as Robert Crumb and Denis Kitchen. Bill came by this influence honestly; his cousin was artist Pete Poplaski, who worked with Kitchen as part of Krupp Comic Works in Princeton, Wisconsin.

Augmento was supposed to return in the fall of 1973, but complaints about sexism led the paper to cancel the strip. Then Mark came along. Fresh off having his comic "Bodi" printed in the *Bugle American*, the Milwaukee-based underground newspaper cofounded by Kitchen, Mark thought *Augmento* had too much potential to be abandoned. So he suggested that he and Bill work on it together as a comic book, with Bill writing and inking and Mark illustrating.

As they began work, they got word that the *Advance-Titan* was interested in bringing the strip back after all. So they reworked their story into fifteen weekly installments, the first of which appeared in the fall of 1974. It would be the first of several times in Mark's career where he would take a concept created by someone else and make it completely his own.

Though *Augmento*, with its experimental style and satirical bent, still had the feel of an underground comic, Mark's artwork—influenced most by Neal Adams, Gil Kane, and Gene Colan—was much slicker and more traditionally superheroic than Bill's. Mark also brought a sense of showmanship to the promotion of the strip. He created posters declaring "Augmento Lives!" and put them up all over campus. And as the comic built up to a battle between Augmento and an armored villainess named Iron Maiden, Mark used the campus radio station and weekly TV show to hype a real-life battle at the school's football stadium after the homecoming parade in October 1974. With Norma's help he sewed costumes for both characters so they could appear in the parade and stage photos of the fight itself. The latter were printed in the *Advance-Titan*, along with the dubious claim that 9,900 people showed up to watch.

When *Augmento* returned in January 1975, Mark had taken over completely (Bill had transferred to Mankato State University). In this second fifteen-part series, *Augmento* featured fussy but innovative layouts, puns and wordplay (after throwing a book at another character, Augmento brags that he has "perfect pitch"), lots of Gruenwald easter eggs (a character wearing a Captain America shirt; a poster for *Icarus* in the background), and a story about Augmento fighting a religious cult overtaking the campus. Mark gleefully incorporated actual people from UW-O into the strip, from cafeteria workers to professors to fellow students. Roy Hoglund says the *Advance-Titan* was never more popular than when Mark was doing *Augmento*. "People couldn't wait to see if they were in there!"

As this series of *Augmento* wrapped up in spring of 1975, Mark seemed to take stock of the work he'd done, and to respond to the critical feedback he'd received. In a parody called "De Mento," the

A poster created as part of Mark's marketing blitz for *Augmento*, 1974. Courtesy of Catherine Schuller.

title character confronts his deadliest enemy, M*rk Gruenw*ld, saying, "Your confusing stories and drawings are killing me!" In the next *Augmento*, Mark wrote himself into the strip to perform a critical evaluation of his own work. As Augmento lists the loose ends and inconsistencies of the story, Mark's comic counterpart patiently addresses them one by one. This practice of addressing questions about and criticisms of his work head on is something Mark would carry with him into his professional career.

In the fall of 1975, Mark's final semester, he brought *Augmento* back for one last fifteen-episode run, this one coplotted with his friend J. Mark Madison. The final series featured simplified layouts, and the introduction of several new heroes and villains, including Blue Streak (a naked speedster with a lightning bolt painted on his chest), Leotard the Dance Master (a nod to Terpsichore), and the Gay Blade (whom Mark based on Roy, after seeing him in a musketeer costume). In the final *Augmento* Mark once again wrote himself into the strip. When Augmento laments that Mark never let him win a single fight, Mark assures him that his troubles are over: "Yep, I've graduated. I'm off to the jungle of New York to become a professional comic booker."

Augmento responds with joy, "I can win fights . . . chase women . . . tell jokes . . . go out drinking . . . I can act out of character!" But as he celebrates the character gradually disappears over the final three panels.

Mark would later look back on *Augmento* with fondness, as a formative experience in learning what works and doesn't work in comics. "I tried some things with it I wouldn't try now," he said in 1979. "If anything, comics should be understood at a glance."

✎ ✎ ✎

Mark graduated college with honors in December 1975, and set about finding a way to break into comics. By that time, he'd already made several connections that would eventually help guide him to a breakthrough.

In high school, Mark had several letters see print in various Marvel and DC comics, and these give insight into just how deeply he thought about every aspect of comics creation, including story, art, and design. In *Daredevil* #40 (May 1968), Mark praised the book as "Marvel's best publication," singling out the plotting, realism, and artwork. He also showed signs of an obsession with consistency (asking how Daredevil was able to get past the Baxter Building's vaunted defenses) and a concern with aesthetics (he suggested the cover logo feature only the character's name).

Mark's letters also demonstrated his already sharp instinct for story. In *Wonder Woman* #181 (April 1969), he praised the new direction of the book under Dennis O'Neil and Mike Sekowsky, in which Diana gives up her powers and costume. Mark suggested that "Wonder Woman becomes a non-super-powered agent of justice, dressed in mod clothes, rather than a uniform, and devoted to breaking up spy rings and battling down-to-earth foes." In response, the editor called him "somewhat psychic" because that's exactly the direction O'Neil and Sekowsky were taking the book.

Mark's letters also saw print in *Justice League of America, Uncanny X-Men, Sub-Mariner, Superman's Pal Jimmy Olsen*, and *The Brave and the Bold* around this time, and they all followed similar patterns, with Mark offering earnest criticisms and creative suggestions.

During his college years, Mark's letter writing slowed, likely because he found a different way to engage with comics professionals and fellow fans: conventions. Mark's first con experience was in 1972 in New York City. Started in 1968 by Phil Seuling, the New York Comic Art Convention was held every year around the fourth of July. In 1972 the con happened to coincide with a National Education Association conference that was taking place in Atlantic City. So Mark, Myron, and Norma drove to New Jersey together, and Mark went on to New York City by himself, where he stayed at the "somewhat seedy" Sloane House YMCA on 34th Street.

The convention—held at the Statler Hilton, right across from Penn Station—was a five-day affair, featuring tons of dealers in comics and comic art, and appearances by comics legends such as

Mark (middle) and David Lofvers (right) connected instantly at the 1972 "Julycon." Mark Lawson (left) lost interest in comics soon after. Copyright and courtesy of David Lofvers.

Bob Kane and C. C. Beck. Mark spent $100 the first day on back issues, was thrilled to get a zen archer Green Arrow headshot from superstar artist Neal Adams, and was deeply impressed by Jack Kirby, who made every fan "feel like he really mattered." Mark vowed that if he ever made it to the pros, he'd treat his fans as well as Jack had treated him.

The inner kid who had temporarily given up comics after sixth grade was overjoyed: "I felt vindicated seeing so many people of all different ages and backgrounds who had one thing in common—a love for the comics." It's no surprise then, that Mark formed a fast friendship with David Lofvers, a DC enthusiast from Rochester, New York. David and Mark met on the second day of the con, and Mark even convinced David and his friend Mark Lawson to check out of their hotel and come over to the Y, using the money they'd save to buy more comics. The trio spent the next three days together. Mark later wrote that it was "a nearly mystical experience to be able to talk constantly about my favorite subject." It was the beginning of a friendship that would endure for the rest of Mark's life.

Concurrent with the rise of conventions was the proliferation of fan-produced comic book magazines and reference guides. Jerry Bails, a natural science professor living in Detroit, was a key figure in this, having cofounded *Alter Ego* with Roy Thomas, and the first nationally distributed fanzine, *The Comic Reader*. But it was Bails's research on the early stories of the Justice Society of America, in 1962's *An Authoritative Index to All-Star Comics*, that truly inspired Mark. Already an obsessive collector and organizer of comic book facts and figures, he decided to create his own version of Bails's index, one focused on his beloved JLA.

The Complete Justice League of America Reader was the result. With Lofvers's help on research and proofreading, Mark self-published the twenty-three-page fanzine in 1973. It included a section with biographical and statistical data on each JLA member, a categorical breakdown of each story by its major plot element, lists of which team members appeared most in the book and on its covers, and summaries and credits for the team's first twelve years of adventures, all under a cover drawn by Mark himself.

In his prologue to the reader, Mark wrote, truthfully but amusingly, that he'd been working on the book since childhood. He also analyzed the major trends and developments of the series, as well as the styles of its writers. He charged that JLA originator Gardner Fox was a plot-driven writer who "seemed to think in terms of super-powers belonging to characters rather than characters who happened to have super-powers." He said that in contrast, Dennis O'Neil (who took over from Fox with issue #68) brought the heroes to life and gave them personality. Mike Friedrich's stories, he wrote, usually had "some ulterior moral or message" that early on in his run was "heavy-handed and obvious." Just like his letters, Mark's work in *The Complete Justice League of America Reader* showcased just how comprehensively Mark thought about superhero comics, and how seriously he took both the work of making them and the integrity of the worlds they depicted. Mark placed an ad for one dollar in the *The Buyer's Guide* and got 250 orders of *The Complete Justice League of America Reader* at fifty cents apiece.

The cover of *The Justice League of America Reader*, 1975. Courtesy of Catherine Schuller.

After that first convention in 1972, Mark started taking regular trips to New York. Typically he'd take a bus to David Lofvers's home in Rochester, and the two would take the ten-hour train ride into the city. Mark would bring along his "Idea Book," which was packed with sketches, scripts, and character concepts. He loved talking through these ideas with David, and getting feedback

Mark was an early contributor to U of W-O classmate Dave Truesdale's science fiction fanzine, *Tangent*. Courtesy of Dave Truesdale.

from his friend. The pair not only attended more conventions, but also made a visit to the DC offices where they got an audience with Julius "Julie" Schwartz, an editor who had been key in the Silver Age revitalization of DC's superheroes, including coming up with the idea for the JLA. Schwartz gave Mark and David some older comics they were missing from their collections, and listened to some of Mark's story ideas, ultimately telling him they weren't commercial enough. They also met with art director Carmine Infantino, who suggested Mark consider applying for the "Junior Woodchucks" an editorial internship program at the company. Mark desperately wanted to do it, but knew he should finish college first.

It was with this in mind when, not long after graduating college, Mark took another trip to New York City, this time to show work samples to Schwartz. He had put most of his focus on working at DC because he felt strongly that the company had "seldom done justice to most of its characters." He had reason to be optimistic. Mark had recently submitted a design for a new header for the *Justice League of America* letters page. It was accepted, adapted by *JLA* artists Dick Dillin and Tex Blaisdell, and debuted in issue #129 (April 1976).

But the meeting with Schwartz ended in a brutal rejection. Schwartz looked over some Augmento pages, and took a cursory glance at a story titled "Vengeance of the Other Joker," and was immediately dismissive. He said Mark's artwork didn't fit DC house style, and made a dubious claim that the Joker idea was duplicative of another story already in the works; no such story ever appeared. "It was also immediately apparent," Mark wrote later, "that they wanted someone who could work within the conventional methods of storytelling, not someone out to expand its conventions."

Mark spent a couple of months back home working up a new portfolio with Schwartz's criticisms in mind, and returned to New York in April 1976. This time he met with Neal Adams, who told him his work had potential, but that he wasn't likely to get a job in comics unless he moved to New York. On the basis of that advice, Mark made the most fateful decision of his life. In early summer of 1976 he left Wisconsin, and headed east to follow his dream.

CHAPTER 3

Into the Omniverse (1976–1978)

> Fictional reality is the oxymoronic name I coined for a literary world's phenomenology: its history, its science, its cosmology, and how that cosmology is systematically related to other literary worlds' cosmologies.
> —Mark Gruenwald, 1994

Mark's first months in New York were both a thrill and a struggle. He had no job and about six hundred dollars in savings. He shared a studio apartment with Bronx native, and fellow aspiring comic book artist, Martin Berkenwald on the top floor of a brownstone on 76th Street in Manhattan. Rent was about $185 a month. There was no oven, no shower, and the toilet was down the hall. They furnished the place with items they found on the curb. It was a far cry from the comfort of his parents' home in Oshkosh, but that's the way Mark wanted it. In showing his art to professionals, one artist pointedly asked Mark what he would do if he couldn't make comics for a living. Mark said maybe advertising or teaching, and the artist responded, "To make it into professional comics, you must have no viable career alternative to fall back on. If you do, you won't be hungry, desperate, or motivated enough. . . ."

Mark was hungry and desperate, but he still found ways to have fun. He formed a fast friendship with his new neighbor across the hall, Virginia native John Wilburn, and together they got into several "Tom Sawyer-type" shenanigans, including climbing the Soldiers and Sailors Memorial Monument in Riverside Park, and visiting Times Square during the 1977 blackout.

Mark (right) and Roy "Chuck" Hoglund (left) cool off on the roof of Mark's apartment building, July 1976. Courtesy of Roy Hoglund.

The most Gruenwald-esque of these involved going rooftop exploring at night. From the hallway of their building they had access to its roof, and at Mark's urging began expeditions to see how far they could get around the block by jumping, scrambling, and climbing from rooftop to rooftop. "He must have been thinking about Spider-Man," Wilburn says. "It was exhilarating." During one of these journeys, they had to make a jump from a building that was about five feet taller. Mark demonstrated how to do it, taking a graceful leap, grabbing onto a metal railing, and pulling himself up. But on Wilburn's attempt, the railing came loose and swung him out over the street. Mark saved the day by pulling the railing, and his friend, back toward the building.

In addition to contributing to various fanzines, Mark threw himself into the self-publishing arena in those early months in New York, putting out *A Treatise on Reality in Comic Literature (TORICL)*, a ninety-six-page book done in the manner of a doctoral thesis. *TORICL* starts with the premise that works of fiction that feature something that sets them apart from our reality—animals that talk, superheroes, aliens, the Axis winning World War II, for instance—are depictions of parallel dimensions. Further, many of these contain their own parallel dimensions within them, creating a weblike network of fictional realities. The goal of *TORICL*, then, was to "provide a detailed examination of the evolution of the Parallel Dimensions concept and, further, to present a theory that binds all the varied and sometimes conflicting representations of Reality into a single, self-consistent system of universes." He called that system the Omniverse.

In *The Complete Justice League of America Reader*, Mark had spent eight paragraphs discussing DC's then-primary parallel dimension, Earth-Two, and the depiction of interdimensional travel in the annual Justice League/Justice Society team-ups originated by Gardner Fox, concluding that there were still many aspects that hadn't been illuminated yet. En route to the 1974 New York Comic Art Convention with David Lofvers, he had written a ten-page article—"Beyond Earth Two: Parallel Dimensions Explained"—that started that work. *TORICL* was the logical continuation, presenting a scientific and mathematical basis for divergent realities, identifying how they are created, inventing rules for travel between them, and illuminating their relationship to time travel.

The latter was perhaps the most significant idea in *TORICL*. Mark posited that a time traveler's actions in moving either forward or backward in time would not change the main reality line, but instead create a new divergent reality line. He offered this colorfully macabre example: "Killing one's grandfather would only produce a new Reality Line in which one has no dimensional counterpart ... it will do nothing to affect one's reality, only one's conscience."

TORICL was esoteric and dense, but Mark illustrated his ideas with a catalog of parallel Earths and characters, a bibliography of comics that relate to alternate realities, and case studies. And while it's not an easy read, it does have some dry wit, as when Mark writes of 1976's *Superman vs. The Amazing Spider-Man*: "Stories like this set back the layman's understanding of Reality many years."

Mark on the back cover of his *Treatise on Reality in Comic Literature*, 1976. "I wanted identification with my product." Courtesy of Catherine Schuller.

TORICL would stand not only as a foundation for Mark's approach to superhero stories, but also another example of his commitment to treating superhero comics with the same level of gravitas as any other form of literature. It was a bravura synthesis of and expansion upon the work of the likes of Samuel Taylor Coleridge (the willful suspension of disbelief), Jorge Luis Borges ("The Garden of Forking Paths" and "The Aleph"), Larry Niven

("All the Myriad Ways"), Philip Jose Farmer (the six-book World of Tiers series), and David Gerrold (*The Man Who Folded Himself*). In 1977, Mark worked with his father to create *A Primer on Reality in Comic Books*, a "general readers" version of *TORICL*.

Though inspired by DC concepts, *TORICL* was very much in step with Marvel, whose new title *What If...* debuted in late 1976. The book—which took significant moments in Marvel history and imagined an alternate outcome—served as an effective illustration of some of Mark's ideas on parallel realities. Mark had a letter published in the comic's second issue, in which he shared seven ideas for the series. The book's editor called him the "Mad Prophet of the Month" for his prescience, as five of Mark's ideas would become actual issues of *What If...* within its first two years of publication.

Around this time, Mark moved into an apartment on 88th Street with Dean Mullaney. Mark had met and befriended Dean at a New York Comic Art Convention in the midseventies. Whereas Mark's comics keystone had been Gardner Fox's *JLA*, Dean's had been Steve Ditko's *Amazing Spider-Man* and *Dr. Strange*. The pair shared a birthday, one year apart, leading Mark to label them "interdimensional brothers." Dean and his actual brother, Jan, were in the process of creating their own comic book company, Eclipse, and there was a brief discussion of bringing Mark into that partnership. In the end, Mark and Dean decided to create a separate company to publish, as Mark put it, "various encyclopedic and reality-based zines." They called it Alternity Enterprises.

It was around this time that Mark became a member of CAPA-alpha, an exclusive, comics-focused amateur press association whose members (which included future pros such as Mark Evanier, Carl Gafford, and Tony Isabella) contributed to a monthly fanzine compiled by Jerry Bails. Mark's contribution was "Personal Entropy," filled with autobiographical essays, humor, philosophical musings on comics, and original artwork and comics stories by Mark and various friends. Mark would produce twelve issues of "Personal Entropy" in total.

Meanwhile, Mark continued to try to get his foot in the door at either Marvel or DC. He trooped into both publisher's offices, relying on the connections he'd made at various conventions, to let them know he was now a New York resident. At Marvel—where he met with new editor-in-chief Archie Goodwin and an assistant editor named Ralph Macchio—there were no openings.

At DC, he met with Denny O'Neil and Paul Levitz. Mark had previously interviewed Levitz at a convention, and had impressed the editor with the depth and breadth of his knowledge of DC characters and storylines. So Levitz hired Mark to write an article for the *Amazing World of DC Comics*. Published in #13 (October 1976), Mark's article—titled "The Martian Chronicles: Chapter Three in the Continuing Guide to Confusing Continuity"—took on the history of the Martian Manhunter, detailing the inconsistencies in his origins, powers, and background that had piled up since the character's first appearance in 1955. Though Mark knew these were all attributable to writers and editors who were unconcerned with internal consistency, he spent the entire last page of the three-page piece detailing his own in-story explanations for the plot holes and contradictions.

Next, Levitz gave Mark the green light to do an official, expanded version of *The Complete Justice League of America Reader*, the results of which appeared in *Amazing World of DC Comics* #14 (March 1977). Mark was given access to all of DC's resources, allowing him to include a detailed schematic of the team's headquarters, create an official team charter, and to conduct a print interview with Julie Schwartz. The latter is a fascinating insight into Mark's attitudes about comics editing.

Mark and Schwartz didn't see eye to eye on fan input (Schwartz regarded letter writers as a vocal minority) or fans-turned-writers' obsession with continuity and consistency (Mark stated that consistency between stories made them more believable and enjoyable, but Schwartz said he didn't feel writers or editors needed to be beholden to stories that were ten or twenty years old). One area of agreement between the two was that the ideal editor/writer relationship included a healthy amount of creative collaboration.

Mark's work on *The Amazing World of DC Comics* was the highest-profile entry yet in the writing and editing résumé he'd had been steadily building since junior high. While Mark's early attempts to break into comics had focused on art, it was likely around this time that he realized that writing and editing represented his best chance. This was cemented with a November 1976 pilgrimage to Yonkers to the home of his writing hero, Gardner Fox. "A kinder, more indulgent man would be hard to find," Mark wrote of the visit. "He did not so much as wince as I tried in my tongue-twisted fashion to express how much his work had meant to me." After sitting in the sixty-five-year-old writer's study and listening to his reminiscences, Mark saw his own future as a comic book writer.

Working for DC may have been highly encouraging to Mark, but it wasn't lucrative. He'd later say he made about five hundred dollars from the work. After about six months in New York with no sign of a full-time job in comics, Mark realized he needed to find a reliable source of income. He went to a temp agency that placed him in the filing department at Citibank. Mark would spend a little over a year there.

With actual steady income, Mark was able to save up his money and think more ambitiously about his next self-publishing venture. Mark claimed that the idea for a fanzine centered on parallel dimensions in fiction came to him while he was selling copies of *TORICL* at the New York Comic Art Convention in the summer of 1976 and discussing his theories with fellow fans. "Many ideas were brought forth as well, some that corroborated and some that challenged my own," he'd later write. It occurred to Mark that he should create a forum for these ideas.

The result was *Omniverse*, a fanzine done in the style and tenor of an academic journal. Published in the fall of 1977, it was a culmination of everything Mark had been working toward for the previous year-and-a-half, not only his theories on parallel realities but the connections he'd been making with his fellow fans and aspiring professionals. Contributors to the first issue of *Omniverse* were a mix of people Dean knew and people Mark knew, including Pete Poplaski, Martin Berkenwald, and future professionals Kim Thompson, Robert Rodi, and Jerry Ordway.

In the introduction, Mark stated his intent for the magazine to approach comic books not as an artform or literature, but as literal accounts of events in other universes. *Omniverse* would serve as a "medium of ideas" exploring those other universes' physical and natural laws. The articles in the first issue fulfilled that promise, including an examination of "Micro-Worlds" (the realms of Ant-Man and the Atom) and a convincing argument for why Howard the Duck couldn't possibly have originated from Disney's Duckburg. Mark himself wrote a piece with the goal of identifying the possible divergent factors between the reality lines of DC's Earth-One and Earth-Two. He also reviewed some recent comics through the lens of their "intrinsic consistency, extrinsic continuity, and whether or not [they] fit into the Omniversal Theory." He gave highest marks to *What If...* #3 (a Jim Shooter/Gil Kane Avengers story) and *Superboy* #223 (a Jim Shooter/Mike Grell story featuring the Legion of Super-Heroes), calling the latter "one of the most intelligent time travel stories in comics history."

Mark and Dean printed 4,000 copies of *Omniverse* #1, and ran out of them in six months. *Omniverse* had been a labor of love, but Mark also realized it could serve as a résumé. "I made sure everyone important in the comics business got a free copy," Mark later revealed. One of those "important people" was Marvel's Roger Stern, with whom Mark had worked on permissions for the magazine.

Stern showed *Omniverse* to Jim Shooter. The twenty-six-year-old Shooter already had a long list of comic-writing credits, and was at that point working as assistant to Archie Goodwin. When Goodwin resigned his post as editor-in-chief at the end of 1977, Shooter ascended to the top spot. The resultant shuffling of personnel created openings in editorial at Marvel. Having been impressed by Mark's production, editorial, and design skills on

The cover to *Omniverse* #1, drawn by Pete Poplaski, 1977. Courtesy of Catherine Schuller.

Omniverse, Shooter called Mark into Marvel's offices. In that interview, Shooter admitted that continuity was one of his weak points, and that he could use someone who knew Marvel history very well.

Though he had read Marvel comics nearly from the start, Mark was not as well-versed in their history as he was in DC's. But he knew Dean had a complete run of Marvels he could use to give himself a crash course, so he told Shooter to look no further.

Mark walked out of the Marvel offices that day with an assistant editor job.

✒ ✒ ✒

Mark's first day at Marvel was February 13, 1978. He was the fourth assistant editor on staff, joining Mary Jo Duffy, Ralph Macchio, and Jim Salicrup. Marvel's editorial structure was in a strange configuration in those days, mostly owing to the tumultuous stretch of time in which the company ran through five editors-in-chief between 1972 and 1977. When Roy Thomas stepped down in 1974, he remained with the company and became a "writer/editor," meaning, essentially, that he edited his own work. This created a precedent, so when Len Wein stepped down as editor-in-chief, he became a writer/editor as well. Same for Marv Wolfman, Gerry Conway, and Archie Goodwin. Even *Howard the Duck* cocreator Steve Gerber got the designation, despite not having been editor-in-chief.

That meant Marvel didn't have traditional editors, nor the consistent oversight and constructive creative struggle that comes from a good working relationship between a writer and an editor. As editor-in-chief, Jim Shooter took it upon himself to reign in the writer/editors, and he used assistant editors as liaisons in that process. That was the role Mark stepped into, and it meant that he was now working with Gerber, Goodwin, Thomas, and Wolfman.

It wasn't easy. As Mark later joked, "I got to learn at their feet while they were stepping on me." But he received a swift education in nearly every aspect of creating comics. Mark read and responded to reader mail, proofread the copy before lettering, helped design covers, and worked closely with the production department. By the end of 1979, Mark would have a hand in twelve of the fifty titles Marvel was producing, including *Fantastic Four*, *Thor*, and *What If....*

Jim Shooter served as Mark's most consistent mentor during this time. Shooter was only two years older, but he had a wealth of experience, and his philosophy of comic book editing would form the foundation for Mark's approach. Like Julie Schwartz, Shooter viewed the role of editor as "part business, part creative." The editor had to coordinate all the elements to get the comic ready for print, but also to serve as the "publisher's face to the creators" to try to match the creators' vision with that of the company. To him, the latter meant that the editor had just as much influence on what went on the page as the writer and artist did.

In 1980, Mark was assigned to editor Dennis O'Neil, who came to Marvel after a twelve-year stint at DC, where he made a name for himself with defining runs writing *Green Arrow/Green Lantern* and *Batman*. Mark had interviewed the writer for *The Amazing World of DC Comics* #14 (and lightly insulted his work on *JLA* #115 of the title, decrying its "loose characterization and plot holes."). Now they'd be sharing an office, working on a diverse range of books, including *Daredevil*, *Moon Knight*, *Man-Thing*, and *Spider-Woman*. Mark would only work with O'Neil for about a year, but the older editor's keen ability to find the core appeal of existing characters, as well as his devotion to creating new ones, were qualities Mark would later take on in his own editing and writing. O'Neil also had a philosophy of editing that differed from Jim Shooter's. He believed the editor's influence should be invisible, and would have preferred his name not even appear in the credits.

In 1981 Marvel hired Queens native Tom DeFalco away from Archie Comics, where he'd served as both a writer and an editor (and the originator of the beloved Archie digest format). DeFalco took over *Marvel Team-Up*, *Ghost Rider*, and *What If...* from O'Neil, and Mark stayed with the titles, becoming DeFalco's assistant editor. When told of the change, DeFalco responded, "Mark Gruenwald, my assistant? I should be his assistant." DeFalco shared Mark's love for the Marvel foundation built by Lee, Ditko, and Kirby, and a belief in the power of superhero comics to shape young minds. Mark and DeFalco's time as editor and assistant editor only lasted a year, but their partnership would become one of the defining elements of Marvel in the 1980s and 1990s.

CHAPTER 4

Writer and Artist (1978–1984)

> I have too many ideas... if I would have no new ideas after today, it would still probably be three years before I'd use all the ideas I've jotted down.
> —Mark Gruenwald, 1979

Mark didn't have to wait long for his first writing assignment at Marvel. When Marv Wolfman left Marvel for DC, Mark took over writing duties on *Spider-Woman* with issue #9 (December 1978). Artist Carmine Infantino—with whom Mark had met when he was at DC—was the series artist. Spider-Woman had only been around a year, but had a convoluted origin both off and on the page. She was created by Archie Goodwin and Marie Severin at the behest of Stan Lee, who was worried that DC would create a character with the name before Marvel could. Indeed, DC had debuted Power Girl in 1976, four years after the first appearance of Marvel's Power Man. Marvel readers, the majority of them male, derided Spider-Woman as unoriginal.

Mark couldn't control the circumstances of Jessica Drew's creation, but he could try to win fans over with what was in the book itself. One of his main goals was to establish a solid status quo: giving Jessica Drew a job, better defining her powers, and building up a respectable rogues gallery of villains.

It was with the latter that Mark seems to have the most fun. For his first issue he created a horror-themed villain called The Needle, whose modus operandi was to sew his victims' mouths shut. Over the next few issues Mark would introduce the Gypsy Moth and Madame Doll, and a repurposed Brother Grimm. The latter was the first instance of what would become a Gruenwald trademark: Picking elements from mostly forgotten old stories and weaving them into a compelling narrative that also cast a new light on the original story. In this case, he connected Brother Grimm to Mister Doll, an obscure villain who'd appeared once in a 1963 *Iron Man* tale (*Tales of Suspense* #48). Jessica's landlady would turn out to be the villain's wife, Madame Doll.

Mark's work on *Spider-Woman* shows he already had command of a couple of aspects that would become hallmarks of his work. First was his gift for plot structure; each issue featured a main story with a beginning, middle, and end, but also had ongoing subplots that continued throughout. Mark's sensitivity to fan input was also already firmly in place. Having been an outspoken fan himself, he respected that sometimes readers saw the big picture better than editors and writers. In the letter column in *Spider-Woman* #13, Mark thanks a group of four fans for discussing *Spider-Woman* ideas at the Baltimore Con in August 1978. One assumes he asked them what it would take to "fix" the book, and incorporated many of their suggestions.

For all its upsides, Mark's run on *Spider-Woman* did not sell well, and Mark was removed after issue #20. According to Jim Salicrup, "Mark was crushed. He was pouring everything he had into that comic."

Some consolation was the fact that he'd already picked up a second regular writing assignment, cowriting *Marvel Two-In-One* with fellow assistant editor Ralph Macchio. The duo began their run with a six-part epic called "The Pegasus Project." Teamed with artists John Byrne (for issues #53–55) and George Perez (for issues #56–58), the story gave new status quos to both heroes (Thundra, Deathlok, Quasar, Wundarr, Black Goliath) and villains (Klaw, Nuklo, Blacksun the Stellar Man). As Mark put it in a 1988 introduction to a trade paperback collection of the story, these were characters that "we could really do something with since no one else had any interest in them." There were even new names for Wundarr (Aquarian) and Black Goliath (Giant Man).

The Thing approves of Giant Man's new codename in *Marvel Two-In-One* #55, 1979. Art by John Byrne, Joe Sinnott, and Bob Sharen. Copyright Marvel Comics.

Following "The Pegasus Project," Mark and Ralph took over as the regular series writers and became known as the "Two-In-One Twins." Their subsequent work on the title remained ambitious, introducing subplots, a recurring supporting cast, and further changes in status quo, all things that had been previously avoided on team-up books. Mark and Ralph would stay on the book—either working together or individually—for nearly two years. They did such memorable stories as "The Coming of Her" and "The Serpent Crown Affair," with art provided by the likes of George Perez, Jerry Bingham, Ron Wilson, and Gene Day.

As they were working on *Marvel Two-In-One*, Mark and Ralph also took over as series writers for *The Mighty Thor* with issue #299 (September 1980). They inherited the job of wrapping up Roy Thomas's meandering *Celestials* saga, which had been going for sixteen issues. With issue #302, the cowriters—along with artists Keith Pollard and Chic Stone—started to establish a new status quo, stationing Thor on Earth again, and bringing back his human alter-ego Dr. Donald Blake. They moved the book away from the heavy fantasy and mythology elements and toward traditional superheroics. They brought in villains such as Locus the Geometric Man, the Wrecking Crew, and the Dream Demon. And they gave Blake a job at a free clinic to further ground the stories on Earth. But their run was short-lived, lasting only until #307 (May 1981). Mark had now been removed from three consecutive titles.

Mark getting hired at Marvel, combined with Dean Mullaney's move to Philadelphia, spelled the end of Alternity Enterprises as an ongoing concern, though Mark did put out a second issue of *Omniverse* in 1979. More importantly, he found myriad ways to imprint its philosophies into the work he was doing. His desire for consistency and interconnection in the Marvel Universe, as well as his theories about and rules for time travel and alternate realities, all show up repeatedly in his early projects.

Fundamental to Mark's approach was to treat Marvel comics as an ongoing account of real events that happened in some alternate reality. This meant that the writers and artists were transcribers and interpreters of events, not creators of them. This idea was detailed by Dean Mullaney in a piece called "The Imagination Fallacy" in *Omniverse* #1. Mullaney concluded that transcribers occasionally make mistakes, whether due to imprecise insight, subjective bias, or an undisciplined grasp of the process of documenting realities. As both writer and editor, Mark took it upon himself to correct as many of those mistakes, inconsistencies, and confusions as he could and, in the process, connect seemingly disparate story threads.

Perhaps the most significant example of this is the coplotting work Mark did on *Avengers* #185–87 (July–September 1979), the story known as "Yesterday Quest." Starting out with the problem of contradictory accounts of the Scarlet Witch and Quicksilver's origins, Mark and Steven Grant prepared thirty pages of single-spaced research on the elements they wanted to address in their story.

In the process of trying to work out Wanda and Pietro's true origins, Mark and Steven started to see a path forward in the facts established in those older stories. Mark wrote, "Those patterns seemed so obvious (in retrospect) that it was as if the long list of writers of the Wanda-Pietro saga had been guided by an unseen plan throughout their apparently contradictory works. When we were through making connections, deriving chronologies from fragments, and answering our own questions, we found we had a tapestry that added meaning and depth to a number of pivotal and peripheral characters."

With David Michelinie coplotting and scripting, and John Byrne on pencils, the story tied Wanda and Pietro's story into the High Evolutionary and his mountain base—Wundagore (which was a also connection to Spider-Woman's origins)—and a villain called Chthon, whose book of evil spells, the Darkhold, had first appeared in the pages of *Marvel Spotlight*.

Mark and Steven's solution was not exactly simple, but it had an elegance that allowed them to make corrections and connections at the same time. According to their version of the story, Wanda and Pietro's mother had come to Wundagore, given birth to the twins, and then abandoned them. They landed in the custody of Django and Marya Maximoff, who had recently lost their own twin children. Wanda and Pietro's unseen father, who is described as having "special abilities" and a desire to rule the world, is strongly suggested to be Magneto (this would later be confirmed in the 1982 *Vision and the Scarlet Witch* limited series, which Mark edited). This explains the twins' abilities (they're mutants), Pietro's white hair, and their early involvement in the Brotherhood of Evil Mutants.

Mark took a similar approach in a six-part Eternals story as a back-up feature in *What If . . .* #23–28 with Ron Wilson on art. It wasn't a "What If" tale, but a history of the Celestials, Eternals, Deviants, and humankind in the Marvel Universe. Mark's purpose instead was to take Jack Kirby's original series and make extensions, connections, and clarifications. In Mark's story, a group of exiled Eternals become the founders of Titan (and thus the ancestors of Thanos), and their conflict with the Kree leads to the creation of the Inhumans. Mark excelled at weaving together the work of many different creators so it seemed like it was always meant to be part of the same narrative.

Another way Mark addressed consistency in the Marvel Universe was by helping to tie up the loose ends of abandoned storylines.

Defenders #77 (November 1979), which Mark helped Steven Grant plot, gave closure to an offbeat hero called Omega the Unknown, whose 1976 series had been canceled after ten issues with its plots unresolved. Similarly, Mark provided research to writer Bill Mantlo for *ROM* #24 (November 1981), which brought a merciful end to Marv Wolfman's "World's War One" story that had begun two-and-a-half years earlier in the pages of *Nova* #24 (on which Mark had served as assistant editor) and had meandered through eleven issues of *Fantastic Four* (#204–214) without resolution.

In addition to providing corrections, connections, and conclusions, Mark brought Omniversal Theory into the Marvel Universe. In a two-part story in *The Mighty Thor* (issues #281 and #282, March and April 1979; art by Keith Pollard), Mark and Ralph devised a story that not only allowed them to make a transcription correction, but to establish ground rules for time travel and travel to alternate dimensions. To do this, they brought back the Space Phantom, a villain who had debuted all the way back in *Avengers* #2 (November 1963), and tied the character's origins to that of the time- and-dimension traveling Immortus.

They revealed that Immortus's very existence is an "ever-growing tree" of alternate dimensions splitting off from a primary timeline. Because of this, the Time-Keepers (a Mark and Ralph creation) have given Immortus the mission of monitoring all time travel and cleaning up "multiplicities [he] created in former lives." In essence this is establishing that the actions of a time traveler don't change the future, but instead create a new reality. Mark also took the chance to make an adjustment to Mjolnir's powers. In *TORICL*, Mark had written with mild annoyance about the hammer's ability to travel through time, and thus used this story to do away with that particular attribute.

✍ ✍ ✍

Between 1981 and 1984, writing work came to Mark in dribs and drabs. He frequently worked out plots with other writers, typically credited with a "plot assist" or "plot idea." Two frequent collaborators were Steven Grant and Bill Mantlo, with whom Mark worked on *Marvel Treasury Edition* #25 ("Spider-Man vs. the Hulk at the Winter Olympics," released in 1980) and its spiritual follow-up, 1982's *Contest of Champions,* considered by many to be Marvel's first line-wide crossover event. He helped develop the concept for *The Saga of Crystar, Crystal Warrior,* which inspired a short-lived toy line in 1982. In 1982 and 1983 he did three intriguing non-superhero stories in the pages of *Bizarre Adventures*.

Though his freelance writing career had stalled in the early 1980s, Mark's personal life was on the ascent. In May 1981, he married an aspiring opera singer named Belinda Glass.

Mark met Belinda, ironically, thanks to his former girlfriend Holly Lindsay. Holly's roommate at Macalester had grown up with Belinda in Evanston, Illinois. Senior year, Belinda came to St. Paul for a visit. She was finishing up a degree in sociology at Northwestern (after two years at Oberlin College), and planned to move to New York to become a professional singer. Holly had kept in touch with Mark and knew he was also New York–bound. "I know a fun, smart guy who's a little weird and could use some friends in New York," she told Belinda. "You should look him up."

So she did. Mark was initially more interested in Belinda romantically than she was in him. She was unimpressed by his long hair, Captain America T-shirt, and overwhelming aftershave. He seemed to her "a somewhat kooky guy who seemed to spend all of his time tied to his typewriter just writing some stuff or drawing pictures." But eventually Mark won her over, and after about eight months of friendship they became a couple.

Their wedding ceremony took place at the Conservatory Gardens in Central Park. Robert Berson, leader of the Society of Ethical Culture, served as officiant. John Wilburn was his honor attendant. The couple had their honeymoon in the Poconos in Pennsylvania, then began their married life in a small apartment on the Upper West Side in Manhattan.

Mark introduced Son of Santa in *Bizarre Adventures* #32 (February 1983), but the character originated on an envelope Mark sent to David Lofvers. Courtesy of David Lofvers.

Mark and Belinda in the early days of their marriage as captured by David Lofvers, circa 1981. Copyright and courtesy of David Lofvers.

As a writer and editor Mark would occasionally do cover layouts and costume designs, but never any final artwork. That changed when, in 1981, he proposed a limited series starring Hawkeye. Jim Shooter not only approved the project, but suggested that Mark draw it himself. If nothing else, Shooter reasoned, the experience of having to draw his own plots would make Mark a better writer. "I didn't know what he meant at first," Mark admitted, "but I do now. Drawing one of my own plots helped me get a better handle on pacing, story flow, and dramatics." Mark also wondered if Shooter felt guilty for yanking Mark from his writing assignments on *Spider-Woman*, *Marvel Two-In-One*, and *The Mighty Thor*.

Operating from the philosophy that a good limited series should leave its main character transformed, Mark decided to bring in another superhero who would forever change Hawkeye's status quo. He had recently helped Steven Grant to rehabilitate S.H.I.E.L.D. agent Bobbi Morse, a character who had appeared in the pages of *Astonishing Tales* as a love interest for Ka-Zar, and then later in *Marvel Super-Action* in the guise of the Huntress. Since that time, DC already had introduced their own Huntress, so Bobbi needed a new identity. For that, Mark reached back to an idea for a villain he'd created during his *Spider-Woman* run but never got the chance to use, a martial arts expert called Mockingbird. In *Marvel Team-Up* #95 (July 1980), written by Grant with art by Jim Janes, Bobbi Morse became Mockingbird.

Mark wrote, "the idea of a PhD in biology falling for a carnival archer who barely finished high school has a bizarre appeal to me." And indeed, in the final issue of the limited series, Hawkeye and Mockingbird elope. (Mark would later regret having the two characters marry: "Unlike in real life, where marriage can be wonderful and fulfilling and thankfully undramatic, comic book marriages are just about the worst thing you can do to the relative happiness of two characters.")

Mark's main concern with his art on the series was accuracy. He recruited his friend Eliot R. Brown (who hailed from Marvel's production department) to take photos of the tunnels and ramps of the #7 subway line he rode every day (which show up in a battle in issue #3 of the series). It was also important to him that he depict Hawkeye's archery skills accurately, so he did a deep dive on the sport, even taping an archery competition from TV.

While working on *Hawkeye* Mark got waylaid by other artistic duties. After finishing the pencils for Hawkeye #1, Mark wrote and drew *What If...* #32 (April 1982), which examined what might have happened if the Korvac saga from *Avengers* #167–77 had gone differently. Mark also contributed artwork and ideas to *What If...* #34 (August 1982), a parody issue full of silly gags such as "What if Black Bolt Got the Hiccups." Mark wrote and drew *Marvel Team-Up Annual* #5 (November 1982), a sequel to "The Serpent Crown Affair" featuring Spider-Man, the Thing, Scarlet Witch, Quasar, and Dr. Strange. He drew even more characters in the pages of *Incredible*

Hulk #279 (January 1983), which found Marvel's heroes gathering to celebrate the Hulk.

After finishing *Hawkeye*—which was released in 1983—Mark provided layouts for *Questprobe* #1 (August 1984), a promotional tie-in to a computer game. His artwork was inked by the legendary John Romita, whose smooth inks made Mark's work look the best it ever had. Mark likely could have continued to do artwork at Marvel, but there just wasn't enough time in the day, and he recognized his own limitations. In a 1986 interview, Mark quipped: "My feeling on drawing is that if someone can do a better job than myself, they should do it. But if they're going to do worse, I'd rather ruin it myself." When he said this, it had been two years since *Questprobe* #1, which would stand as the last full-length comic featuring Mark's artwork.

CHAPTER 5

Mark the Editor (1982–1987)

> When I was among the riotous ranks of Marvel's rollicking readers, I would muse to myself what a cool fraternity of creative people there was in the comic biz.
> —Mark Gruenwald, 1993

One of the most unique aspects of Mark's early days in comics was that he was part of the first generation of comics professionals who had grown up fans of the characters and books they were working on. Older professionals like Roy Thomas had also been fans when they were young, during what is known as the "Golden Age." Mark and his peers, however, had been there at the forefront of the birth of modern Marvel. They were disciples of Stan Lee and Jack Kirby and Steve Ditko, and that was the lens through which they approached their work. This wasn't just on the pages of the comics themselves, but in their editorial philosophies, how they viewed and interacted with fans, and even in how they approached working in the fabled Marvel bullpen. This was especially true of Mark.

After paying his dues as an assistant editor for nearly four years, Mark became a full-fledged editor in January 1982. He was assigned his own assistant, twenty-three-year-old Mike Carlin, a cartoonist who'd worked on Marvel's version of *Mad Magazine*, *Crazy*. The duo took over the Avengers suite of titles: *Avengers, Captain America, Iron Man,* and *Thor*. Mark was ecstatic to be editing some of Marvel's most iconic characters. To him, *Avengers* was the "quintessential Marvel comic" and the "crossroads of the Marvel Universe."

Though taking over these titles was certainly a huge honor and responsibility, it wasn't quite the plumb assignment it seems now. Both *Captain America* and *Thor* were underperforming, saleswise, to the point of being considered for cancellation. Even *Avengers* had been in a sort of fallow period, with Shooter himself writing the book for a carousel of artists. But Mark wasn't just content to boost sales. He wrote, "My goal is to surpass (or match if the highwater mark was set by guys like Lee and Kirby) the quality and excitement from each of the four Avengers books' top creative periods."

The key to achieving that goal, he reasoned, was to get the right creative teams. For *Iron Man*, the solution was as simple as hiring his former boss, Dennis O'Neil, to helm the book. The result was an acclaimed four-year run, largely with artist Luke McDonnell, that introduced archrival Obadiah Stane and found pilot James Rhodes taking over the identity of Iron Man. When O'Neil left, Mark brought back a team that had worked on the book to great acclaim from 1978 to 1982, David Michelinie and Bob Layton. In their second run they worked with Mark D. Bright to introduce Ghost and the epic Armor Wars storyline.

For *Captain America*, Mark came on at the end of a first year of a run by J. M. Dematteis—on which he worked most frequently with artist Mike Zeck—and decided to let the creative team continue their work. He would oversee two more years until DeMatteis's abrupt departure (see chapter 8).

To chronicle the adventures of the Avengers, Mark brought in Roger Stern, who had transitioned from editing to writing with his work on *Captain America*, *The Incredible Hulk*, *Amazing Spider-Man*, and *Doctor Strange*. Stern, first paired with Al Milgrom and then John Buscema, crafted a nearly five-year run that included what is considered one of the best Avengers stories ever, "Under Siege" (#264–277), wherein the Masters of Evil decimate the World's Mightiest Heroes. They also introduced the California-based West Coast Avengers.

Mighty Thor was the trickiest of the bunch. Mark inherited writer Doug Moench (who had replaced Mark and Ralph on the title) for six issues, then hired Alan Zelenetz and artists Bob Hall and Mark D. Bright. But the title's sales dropped even further, so Mark's Hail Mary to save the book from cancellation was to offer it to writer/artist Walter Simonson, who accepted on the condition he be given carte blanche. Mark wisely agreed, and Simonson promptly set off on what is now considered the definitive run of Thor stories, rivaling the original Lee/Kirby iteration. Combining mythology, superheroics, epic drama, and space opera, he introduced the alien Beta Ray Bill, Malekith the Dark Elf, and Throg the Thor Frog. Sales went through the roof.

Finding the right creative teams for his books was a huge part of Mark's success as an editor, but so was the guidance and support he gave those teams. He started by establishing a common understanding of the core concept of each book and what made it successful. For example, with *The Avengers*, he reread all of the previous issues of the series to determine the team's "standard operating procedure," and then commissioned Stern to write a charter for the team. This was perhaps a sly way to ground his writer in the structured realism Mark so valued.

Mark's overarching editorial philosophy developed from his mentor/apprentice relationships with Shooter, O'Neil, and DeFalco, as well as his years as a fan. In addition to finding the right creative team and determining the fundamental appeal of the book, Mark believed in the editor as organizer, nitpicker, go-betweener, collaborator, and final arbiter.

Part of the job was managerial and technical—coordinating schedules and deadlines; proofreading; creating the letters page; writing cover copy; and more—but that was not the part Mark particularly enjoyed. He did enjoy the responsibility of making sure that his books' story logic, structure, and characterization remained consistent, both with their own pasts and the rest of the Marvel Universe. "What's most important is that a writer stays true to the spirit and basic legend of the character," Mark wrote. "As editor, it's my job to see that he or she stays true to the wealth of sometimes trivial background details."

Mark also served as a go-between, bridging directives from the editor-in-chief and the creative desires of the writer and artist. Mark was a company man and a rule-follower, but he also knew when and how to protect his creative teams. During Dennis O'Neil's *Iron Man* run, the writer wanted to have Tony Stark relapse into alcoholism (as a follow-up to the famous "Demon in a Bottle" storyline from 1979), but Jim Shooter was staunchly against it. Mark, however, fought for his creative team, won, and didn't even let O'Neil know he'd done it. "I later found out that Mark Gruenwald shielded me," O'Neil recalled in 2009.

But what Mark relished most about editing was the opportunity to serve as an integral part of the creative team, both in brainstorming story and character ideas, and in determining the long-term direction of the book. He saw it as his job to ignite his creative teams' excitement, and for many the way to do that was through collaboration.

For the most part, Mark had excellent and productive working relationships with his writers, but there were times when conflict arose. The most significant case of this was in 1987, when Roger Stern balked at a plan to replace Avengers leader Captain Marvel (Monica Rambeau) with Captain America as part of a larger shake-up of the book. Mark's idea was to have Monica make a mistake that called into question her competence. As Rambeau's cocreator, Stern was especially protective of the character, but more than anything feared it would appear both sexist and racist to have a Black female represented as inferior and not up to the job. Mark argued that if the story was done correctly, that criticism would ring hollow.

Mark once wrote, "If there's ever a serious disagreement between a writer and an editor, the editor always wins." This wasn't about ego or hubris—Mark fully accepted that he was subject to this same rule when he was on the writing side of the equation—but the reality in comic books is that the writer is the business providing service to a client, and it's their job to make sure the client is happy. In the case of *Avengers*, Mark decided to go ahead with the storyline as they had coplotted it, replacing Stern with his friend Ralph Macchio. It was a difficult decision to lose a writer he had found to be "dependable, enthusiastic, and meticulous," for the previous five years, but Mark felt it was the right thing to do for the book.

The final component of Mark's editing philosophy was his responsiveness to fans. Mark subscribed to Stan Lee's view of the fan as the true editor, and made every effort to make fans feel as though they had a direct line of communication to him. One of the main ways he did this was with "Mark's Remarks," a column that ran in each of the books he edited. Working under the assumption that readers were following all the titles he edited, Mark wrote three or four different columns each month.

Mark used "Mark's Remarks" to give fans behind-the-scenes access to his thinking, to solicit feedback, give advice, create lists, and stir up controversy. Between June 1986 and January 1989, he wrote ninety-three columns in the pages of *Avengers*, *Iron Man*, *West Coast Avengers*, and *Solo Avengers*. He relished having a forum for open dialogue, but was dismayed that 90 percent of the letters he received were pointing out production mistakes and asking for a famed no-prize (the empty envelope Stan Lee would send out to fans who explained away a mistake), instead of "honest, heartfelt, specific comments" about what fans did and didn't like about the stories themselves. So serious was he about this that he wrote a "Mark's Remarks" column in *Iron Man* #208 (July 1986) declaring he would no longer award no-prizes, and printing a picture of the envelope "to commemorate the passing."

When he did get genuine feedback, both as an editor and writer, Mark took it to heart. For example, when Wonder Man debuted a garish green and red costume in *West Coast Avengers* #12 (September 1986), fan reaction was overwhelmingly negative, so the costume was promptly replaced. Similarly, when Mark floated the idea of changing the title of *West Coast Avengers* to *The New Avengers*, he reported that 95 percent of fans were against it, so the title remained.

When Mark was a young comics reader, he reveled in Stan Lee's portrayal of the Marvel offices and the camaraderie among its staffers. When he began working there himself, he discovered the Marvel bullpen as Stan described it was as much a work of fiction as the books Marvel published. But Mark didn't see any reason that it had to be that way. As Sean Howe wrote in *Marvel: The Untold Story*, Mark was "seemingly determined to will the mythical old Marvel Bullpen—a fantasy realm of practical jokes, crazy nicknames, manic creativity, and cheerful labor—into reality."

Mark brought a mischievous spirit and an infectious "let's put on a show" mentality to work with him each day. His sense of humor—as evidenced by his love of the Three Stooges—tilted heavily toward the lowbrow, absurd, and punny. He reveled in slapstick and pratfalls, the more over-the-top the better. Scatological humor was always funny, especially farts, which Mark called "making air biscuits." Eliot R. Brown recalls that one of the few times he saw Mark truly beside himself with laughter was when he came across a piece of graffiti on a bathroom stall at a rest stop in New Jersey. It read: "Turds over three pounds must be lowered by rope!—Management."

Mark also loved inside jokes, silly words and songs, and pranks, indulging in the latter as often as he could get away with. From rearranging Tom DeFalco's bookshelf whenever he was out of the office to pressing every button in the elevator at 575 Madison to cajoling everyone into wear Groucho glasses on "Shap" day in honor of fellow staffer Barry Shapiro, Mark possessed a bottomless bag of tricks that were guaranteed to sow minor chaos in the office. "Mark believed in fun," wrote Dennis O'Neil of his former assistant. "And when he couldn't find it, he made it."

Mark organized or created games, jokes, outings, pranks, and stunts that were sometimes hilariously surrealistic and sometimes close to spooky. Writer and editor Peter David claims, "No gag was too insane, no joke too juvenile." Mark himself wrote that his first rule of comedy was "Anything more annoying to someone else than it is to you is funny."

Mark balanced his pranks with morale-boosting and community-building activities such as paddleball tournaments, turning his office into a haunted house, and organizing outings to movies, amusement parks, and volleyball games in Central Park. He tried to serve as a force of contagious positivity and joy in the office.

Two disparate projects perfectly illustrate the zany spirit Mark brought to the Marvel offices. His innovative thinking, creative editing, and love of spectacle went into the cover of *Spider-Woman* #50 (June 1983). Ironically, given his removal from the book in 1979, Mark had taken over editorial reigns as the book finished up its run. For the final issue, Mark hatched a plan to create a photo cover featuring Spider-Woman and the characters that had played prominent roles in the title. He recruited friends and Marvel staffers to dress up, including secretary Lynn Luckman as Spider-Woman, series writer Ann Nocenti as Tigra, Belinda in the role of the Gypsy Moth, and Mark himself as Tatterdemalion. Most of the costumes came from Mark's own personal stash of dress-up attire. Eliot R. Brown shot the photo outside Bob Camp and Vincent Waller's studio, and Ron Zalme spent ten days touching it up for publication. The result was one of the most striking and ambitious covers in Marvel's history.

And then came the eight-episode run of *Cheap Laffs*, a 1984 public access television show written by and starring Mark, Mike Carlin, and Eliot R. Brown. Mark funded *Cheap Laffs* himself—including buying a $2,400 camera—and wrote and performed the catchy, punny theme song. Very much in the spirit of *SCTV* and *Monty Python's Flying Circus*, the show featured absurd sketches, fake commercials, and Brown reading the lyrics to sitcom theme songs as if they were poetry. Perhaps the show's most Gruenwald-centric moment was a sketch titled "Living Lifestyles," in which a host interviews a panel of men from various decades. Mark, ensconced in plastic wrap and little else, played Weebwow, a man from the future who answers every question with

Cover of *Spider-Woman* #50, 1983. Copyright Marvel Comics.

David Lofvers (back) visited the *Cheap Laffs* set and took this photo using his camera's self-timer, June 1984. Copyright and courtesy of David Lofvers.

high-pitched gibberish. Several Marvel staffers appeared on the show and were given a chance to shine, including Bob Harras, Jack Morelli, Ann Nocenti, Howard Mackie, John Byrne, and Larry Hama's band The K-Otics.

Mark wasn't content just to bring this spirit of unpredictability, bonhomie, and community to the Marvel offices. He wanted to bring the Bullpen to the fans, and conventions gave him the perfect opportunity to do that. When Mark started at Marvel in 1978 he got to experience going to conventions as a comics pro, and he found it lacking. It seemed mostly to consist of meeting with fans who invariably asked him if he worked on *Uncanny X-Men*, and participating in tedious discussion panels. So just as he did with the Marvel offices, Mark decided to spice things up.

Working with Steven Grant, he devised a series of interactive games and activities for Marvel-led panels, and recruited fellow professionals to participate in them. There was "The Plotting Game," a *Dating Game* take-off where a panel of judges picked the fan who could come up with the best Marvel plot ideas. "Pros and Cons" aped *Hollywood Squares*, and featured the likes of Bill

Sienkiewicz, Len Wein, and Frank Miller as panelists. "Secrets Behind the Comics" was, according to Mark, a series of "well-conceived, poorly executed" performance pieces such as doing an interpretive dance to a beat reading of an issue of *Shogun Warriors*. Another found Belinda coming up on stage to shave off Mark's beard with a straight razor. With his yen for performing, Mark was a natural master of ceremonies for these panels. Eliot R. Brown wrote that, with a deadpan smarminess and midwestern lilt in his voice, Mark's host persona was akin to Barth Gimble, Martin Mull's character on *Fernwood 2 Night*.

As fun as it was for Mark to play the ringmaster at conventions, once he became an editor it became harder to find the time to attend them. His days as a convention trickster were far from over, but they went on pause for about five years. Part of this was family related. Mark and Belinda's daughter, Sara, was born in September 1985. Mark was excited about fatherhood, but Sara's arrival coincided with the busiest time in his career. From 1985 to 1987, Mark was essentially working two jobs. He had a full editorial slate of five titles, plus the not-insignificant additional work of overseeing nearly every aspect of *The Official Handbook of the Marvel Universe Deluxe Edition* and writing multiple "Mark's Remarks" essays each month. On top of this, his writing career had experienced a resurgence in 1985. In addition to a miniseries featuring the Squadron Supreme, Mark became the series writer for *Captain America*.

When Mark took over as the editor of the Avengers-related titles in 1982, *Captain America*—then about one year into a run by writer J. M. DeMatteis and artist Mike Zeck—was the one book he hadn't shaken up. But Jim Shooter had been encouraging editors to push big status quo changes, so Mark and DeMatteis devised a story that would culminate with Steve Rogers being replaced as Captain America by the Navajo hero Black Crow. Shooter, ironically, didn't like this idea and refused to approve it. DeMatteis quit in protest, and Mark was forced to rewrite issue *Captain America* #300 (December 1984), crediting himself under the Monty Python–inspired name Michael Ellis.

Needing a new creative team, Mark offered the book to Tom DeFalco and Ron Frenz, but the duo passed because they were content working on *Amazing Spider-Man*. As Mark made his pitch to DeFalco, sharing his ideas for where the book should go, DeFalco finally said, "Mark, you should be writing the book!" To make that work, Mark had to step down as editor. In the transition, Mike Carlin took over as writer for six issues, then swapped places with Mark, becoming his former boss's editor with issue #307 (July 1985).

A 1986 *Marvel Age* account, "A Day in the Life of Marvel Comics," demonstrates just how busy Mark was during this time. Mark is everywhere in the diary: doing word balloon placements for an issue of *Captain America*, answering editorial questions about *Iron Man* (artist Mark D. Bright wanted to know exactly where Tony Stark was currently living), ironing out a coloring separation snafu on an issue of *West Coast Avengers*, juggling artwork and layout for *The Official Handbook of the Marvel Universe*, conferring with Ralph Macchio about *Squadron Supreme*, and eating lunch with Pete Poplaski's brother, Bill. Since his days were filled with his editing tasks, Mark typically did his writing nights and weekends (often spending five hours each on Saturdays and Sundays). This added up to a situation where there were precious few hours each week during which Mark was not either working or sleeping.

In interviews and essays from this time Mark referred to being overextended and exhausted. In a piece about his New Year's resolutions for 1987, he vowed to spend more time with his family and play more guitar, and warned that if he didn't allow himself more of a break, "Marvel is going to have one burned-out editor." And yet, not six months later he reaffirmed his commitment to editing: "This really is the Glamor Profession," he wrote, "and I wouldn't trade it for any other."

CHAPTER 6

The Official Handbook of the Marvel Universe (1983–1993)

> As far as being a historian, it's not that I know a lot, it's that I care a lot.
> —Mark Gruenwald, 1987

Mark was not in any way a sports enthusiast, but he surely felt an affinity with fans of America's national pastime. Like comics readers, baseball obsessives follow the escapades of colorfully garbed athletes and are collectors of historical and statistical trivia. A primary difference, however, was that baseball fans had a built-in way to collect and categorize information about their heroes; baseball cards had been around almost as long as the game itself. Superhero comic readers had no equivalent way to keep track of the multitude of characters in the Marvel and DC universes.

This frustrated Mark, and projects like *The Complete Justice League of America Reader* and his 1978 self-published *Jack Kirby's New Gods Index* were attempts to create such resources himself. Eliot R. Brown wrote, "Mark had been organizing, collating, tabulating and cross-referencing comic characters and stories since his childhood. . . . It could be said he spent a leeetle [sic] bit too much time on such things. . . ."

This was one of the reasons he connected so well with Dean Mullaney, who had used index cards to make character profiles for every single character who'd ever appeared in a Marvel comic. Formalizing their efforts to create what they called *Who's Who* guidebooks was one of the goals that had driven the formation of

Alternity Enterprises. Mark wrote of his desire for such resources in an essay called "What Fankind Needs," published in the fall/winter 1978 issue of the fanzine *Woweekazowie*. Here he said that the superhero genre was missing "hard, basic research about comics . . . a compilation of data . . . comprehensive indexing and summarizing and cataloging about every aspect of the comics medium and what it depicts, in an accessible format that will enable all to use it for whatever purpose."

He went on to outline four specific projects he'd like to see, one of which was "a complete character index to every entity in both DC and Marvel universes." He explained that "each entity would be cross-referenced to its every appearance and would have biographical data." He concluded, "Yes, it's one hell of a project, but it's going to *have* to be done someday. . . ."

By the time that essay was published, Mark was already working for Marvel. He didn't waste time proposing his idea, but the project didn't get any traction at first. Undeterred, Mark began laying the groundwork by peppering his various books with "data" about its characters and concepts. In *Spider-Woman* #11 (1979) he included a one-pager explaining the character's powers. In *Thor* #303 (1980) a back-up titled "The Legendary Gods of Asgard" featured character pin-ups by Keith Pollard with brief text descriptions and a listing of their first appearances. In *Amazing Spider-Man Annual* #15 (1981) he wrote and drew a back-up titled "Just How Strong Is Spider-Man?," which sorted Marvel heroes into five strength categories.

The latter feature had gotten an overwhelmingly positive response from fans, and that got the attention of Jim Shooter. This, in conjunction with Shooter happening across a battleship schematics book called *Jane's Fighting Ships*, led the editor-in-chief to propose a Marvel specifications book that would present vital statistics (height, weight, strength, and so on) for its major characters. Roger Stern suggested the title "Super-Specs."

In the meantime, Mark had continued to send out test balloons for a Marvel "complete character index," most notably in the *Contest of Champions* limited series, which devoted two pages in each issue to a back-up feature called "Marvel Superheroes—1982." This consisted of an alphabetical listing of characters, including secret identities, descriptions, current whereabouts, and first appearances. *Contest of Champions* #3 listed "Inactive Superheroes and Honor Roll of the Deceased," "Superheroes of Other Worlds, Other Times" and "Quasi-Heroes." This format, combined with Shooter's specifications idea, resulted in a green light for *The Official Handbook of the Marvel Universe* (*OHOTMU*).

The first thing Mark did was assemble a team. His primary partner was researcher Peter Sanderson, a walking Marvel encyclopedia with whom Mark had worked on *Omniverse*. They were joined by freelance writers Peter B. Gillis, Mike Carlin, and Eliot R. Brown. The group started by devising a list of characters they felt should appear in *OHOTMU*.

After finalizing the categories of information to include, the team divvied up the characters and began the process of researching. Sanderson and Gillis both had a level of knowledge of Marvel history that outstripped Mark's, but Mark insisted that all of the information come with textual proof from the comics themselves. When it came time to write the entries, Mark and Sanderson each took half.

Mark and Mike were in charge of creating the visual layout of the project. When Marvel moved into new offices at 387 Park Avenue South in May 1982, they came outfitted with walls covered entirely in corkboard. Mark and Mike used those walls to lay out each issue of *OHOTMU*. In addition to the text, each entry was to have a brand-new illustration, so Mark and Mike commissioned work from a wide variety of artists, including John Byrne, Paul Smith, Walt Simonson, and Kerry Gammill. Eliot took care of typesetting, and also provided scientific and mechanical consultation.

Mark knew *OHOTMU* was a massive undertaking, but still completely underestimated the amount of time and work that would be required. It took the team seven weeks to finish the first issue, which was released with a cover date of January 1983. But the title was due to come out monthly, so they knew spending that much

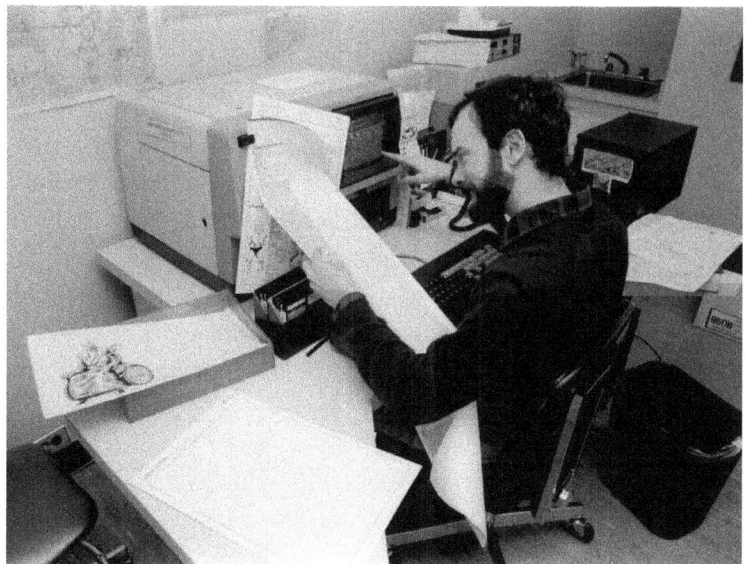

Mark hard at work on *OHOTMU*, circa 1983. He loved using the word processor in Eliot Brown's typesetting office. Courtesy of Eliot R. Brown.

time per issue was untenable. They managed to shave their work time down to the necessary 3.5 weeks per issue, but not without great sacrifice. Work on *OHOTMU* often started after everyone had fulfilled their daily duties, which meant they worked through the nights and weekends. As Eliot put it, the key to finishing *OHOTMU* without ever missing a deadline was "long hours, no showers" and that his personal record was a 153-hour work week. The guys kept themselves going with air-popped popcorn and occasional trips to Smiler's Deli for a 2:00 a.m. meal.

As an editor, Mark was salaried and didn't get any extra pay for his efforts. Even more astonishing is that Mark did this while also writing and drawing the four-issue *Hawkeye* miniseries and editing the monthly *Avengers, Iron Man, Thor,* and *Captain America* titles. But the result was the fulfillment of Mark's dream of an official catalog of Marvel's characters.

And it wasn't just that. Over its initial fifteen-issue run, *OHOTMU* also included maps of key places; building blueprints;

schematics of weapons, vehicles, and other items (both technological and magical); and a complete listing of the known alien races in the Marvel Universe. For the detail-minded fan, it was nirvana. For Mark, it was another chance to honor what Stan Lee, Jack Kirby, Steve Ditko, and the early Marvel staff had created. "The basic believability of the Marvel Universe," he wrote in an editorial in the first issue, "enables us to be very precise about our facts and figures." And to later criticisms that defining things so specifically put limits on writers and artists, Mark responded, "What it boils down to is this: our entries describe the known, they don't limit the unknown."

Mark and his team ran into some interesting conundrums in putting *OHOTMU* together. Though the philosophy of the team was to always rely on the text, there were times the comics presented contradictory information. This allowed Mark to indulge one of his favorite pastimes: "smoothing over the rough patches and inconsistencies" of Marvel's history by looking at all of the accounts, finding which were "at variance" and determining the most likely truth. This went hand in hand with Mark's view of continuity problems as "errors in translation" made by writers and artists. He hoped that writers and other editors would use the handbook themselves, and perhaps avoid some of those errors in the future.

When the team discovered missing information—such as a character's place of birth or real name—they went to the editor or writer to fill in the blanks. In the cases of the books that Mark wrote, he was allowed to make the decision himself. So he gave Constrictor and Sidewinder hometowns in Wisconsin (Kenosha and Racine, respectively). And he made Hawkeye hail from Waverly, Iowa. One supposes the fact that Iowa is the "Hawkeye State" dictated that part of the choice, but Mark's personal touch was choosing Waverly, where his parents had gotten married. Mark also paid homage to one of his favorite TV shows by giving Baron Von Strucker the alias of Don Guy Antonio Caballero, after Joe Flaherty's *SCTV* character Guy Caballero.

When all the work was over, Mark had the entire set bound into books for himself, Mike, and Eliot. In gilded letters on the cover he gave it the title "The Year of Living Stupidly." Mark would later remark that OHOTMU was "the most difficult editorial package ever produced in comics."

The response to OHOTMU was phenomenal, both in sales and in reader mail, especially considering, as Mark pointed out, it didn't even have a letters page. Fans wrote in with praise and with corrections. The mistakes rankled Mark, but even he had to admit that some of them were pretty funny, such as when the villain the Wizard was listed as having been a "stage musician" instead of a "stage magician."

And as the saying goes, imitation is the sincerest form of flattery, so Mark must have been thrilled in 1985 when Marvel's main rival used OHOTMU as the basis for their own character catalog, and even took Mark and Dean's original name, calling it *Who's Who: The Definitive Directory to the DC Universe*. Though it was visually more appealing than OHOTMU, the content of DC's version was almost identical in format and content. Mark would even contribute artwork for the profile of the villain Merlyn in *Who's Who* #15 (May 1986).

OHOTMU's original fifteen-issue run was just the beginning. Its success made a continuation of the project inevitable, but so did its very nature. As Mark wrote in *Marvel Age* #24, "The moment you put it down, more things happen, and your data has become outdated." In addition to reflecting those changes, the deluxe edition of OHOTMU, which began publishing in December 1985, allowed Mark to refine the formula. The issues were twice as long, allowing Mark and his team to give characters longer entries, increase the type size, incorporate Brown's "weapons, hardware, and paraphernalia" schematics into the entries, and include artwork taken from the comics themselves.

Though making the deluxe version of OHOTMU didn't require the insane hours that the original had, it was still a nearly overwhelming amount of work. And now that he was also writing two monthly books, Mark's plate was even fuller than it had been before. With issue #14 (January 1987), he reduced *OHOTMU* from a monthly to a bimonthly "to avoid terminal burn-out by yours truly and staff." In the end, though, Mark felt that the deluxe edition blew the original away, especially when the twenty issues of this run were collected into a series of ten trade paperbacks. Fans agreed, and the series sold even better than the first had by a significant margin.

In the ensuing years, *OHOTMU* continued to thrive. Mark was largely uninvolved with the eight-issue *Update '89*, which featured characters who had either debuted or changed significantly since the deluxe edition. His former assistant editor Gregory Wright took over as editor (he wrote in the first issue that "this book always was [Mark's] 'baby' and so he probably will be looking in with some kind of pathetic look of longing"), and Peter Sanderson handled the researching and writing. The format was the same as the deluxe edition.

In 1990, Mark came back to *OHOTMU* for what was dubbed the "Master Edition." This featured a collection of loose-leaf, three-hole-punched cards with front, side, and back views (all done by Keith Pollard and Josef Rubenstein) on the one side and textual information on the other. Mark edited the series for its first year, in addition to contributing to both the research and writing of the entries. Each set featured a random assortment of twenty-five character sheets that fans could collect and organize by whatever system they wished. Mark wrote that the new modular format would "enable us to update this indefinitely without having to start all over from the beginning of the alphabet."

The Master Edition was originally slated to be part of an ambitious expansion and deconstruction of *OHOTMU*. Acknowledging that the original tried to be a lot of things at once, Mark planned several spin-offs, including a new Marvel Technical Manual, a Marvel Database (an alphabetical index to character appearances), and a Tourists' Guide to the Marvel Universe, but none of these ever saw the light of day. As it was, the Master Edition lasted three years and thirty-six "issues."

OHOTMU would return periodically in subsequent years, most notably in 2004 and 2010, and its format is cemented as the standard way Marvel communicates information about its characters. In fact, Marvel.com profiles of their characters include a narrative biography, statistical information such as height, weight, aliases, and known relatives, and a 0–10 scale of their physical abilities.

Besides being yet another example of the way in which Mark permanently altered the landscape of the Marvel Universe, *OHOTMU* was a significant victory in Mark's ongoing crusade for consistency. It was also a testament to his work ethic, his love of collaboration, and his uncanny ability to find coconspirators to match his energy and intensity to carry out a project. Eliot R. Brown wrote, "It was Mark who assembled this never-to-be-done-again team of brilliant thinkers, workers and artisans. This was a point in Marvel's and comics in general's history where it was possible to drive forward such a project and pay for it. That was dumb luck or inspired genius on Mark's part. I say genius. There were lots of people listed in the credits but it was Mark who was the lighthouse lamp in the dark."

CHAPTER 7

Squadron Supreme (1985–1989)

> Before I leave this business, I'd like to do all the things I've wanted to see done with comics. The subject matter can be of a greater variety.
> —Mark Gruenwald, 1979

In the nearly forty years since its release, the twelve-issue *Squadron Supreme* limited series—done with artists Bob Hall, John Buscema, and Paul Ryan—has come to be regarded as Mark's definitive statement on superhero teams and a blueprint for modern comic book writing. But when he wrote *Squadron Supreme*, Mark was not—for once—trying to create a treatise. His primary goal was to do things that had never before been done in superhero comics, and there were a variety of factors that allowed him to do just that.

It all started with the Squadron Sinister, a tongue-in-cheek parody of the Justice League of America that first appeared in *Avengers* #69 (October 1969). Created by Roy Thomas and Sal Buscema, the team consisted of other-dimensional analogues to Superman (Hyperion), Batman (Nighthawk), Green Lantern (Doctor Spectrum), and the Flash (the Whizzer). In *Avengers* #85 (February 1971), Thomas and John Buscema introduced their heroic counterparts, the Squadron Supreme. The team appeared a few times over the years, including a multi-issue 1975 *Avengers* storyline by Steve Englehart and George Perez that expanded the roster to include homages to Green Arrow (called Hawkeye at first, later the Golden Archer), Black Canary (Lady Lark), Hawkman (Blue Eagle), and the Atom (Tom Thumb).

The fact that the Squadron Supreme characters were initially created as DC analogues was both important and not important to the series' creative success. Mark's long-standing love and encyclopedic knowledge of the JLA gave a poetic resonance to him becoming the writer to take possession of their Marvel equivalents. He clearly relished that aspect, even giving the president-elect of the U.S. the name Jules Gardner, after JLA creators Julie Schwartz and Gardner Fox. But at the same time, the story works equally well on its own for a reader that has none of that knowledge.

Before Mark's limited series, the Squadron Supreme characters were little more than names and costumes, with next to no individuality or history. As Mark put it, "The Squadron used to be characterized by the fact that they didn't really have personalities. At least not consistent ones." So over the *Squadron Supreme* series, Mark imbued each of the characters with life, giving them quirks, foibles, and backstories that set them apart from their DC counterparts. He did a lot of this work efficiently in the first issue, with one-page vignettes that provided readers with more information about the characters than all of their previous appearances combined. He continued this through the series. As reviewer Markalan Joplin wrote in a review at the time, the series is filled with "charming, human moments that provide a welcome respite from the usual tidal wave of trumped-up angst that pervades most team books."

In a 1986 interview, Mark would divulge that moving the characters away from their origins was done partly out of necessity, because DC had threatened a lawsuit when they got wind of the *Squadron Supreme* series. Though Marvel was protected because DC hadn't taken legal action when the characters first appeared in 1969, it was in everyone's best interest not to push the JLA parallels.

So while some of the dozen or so new characters he introduced in the series have analogues at DC (Shape is akin to Elongated Man, Moonglow has the same powers as Gypsy), the majority don't. Mark had actually been doing this sort of reclamation and reformation work since his early days at Marvel. The Shroud—a

The Squadron Supreme appeared on the cover of *Amazing Heroes* #70 (May 1985), depicted by Bob Hall and John Beatty. Courtesy of Fantagraphics Books (www.fantagraphics.com).

character Mark brought into *Spider-Woman*, and about whom he wrote a moody black-and-white short story for *Marvel Preview* #21 (May 1980)—was created by Steve Englehart as a Batman pastiche. Wundarr, whose transformation into the Aquarian was a vital element of "The Pegasus Project," had started out as an exploration of what would have happened to baby Kal-El if he hadn't been found by Jonathan and Martha Kent.

Before Mark took over the Squadron's adventures, their final appearance had been in a 1982 *Defenders* storyline by J. M. DeMatteis and Don Perlin. In this tale set in the Squadron's reality, a mind-controlling villain called the Overmind has taken over the US government. The Squadron breaks his hold, but only after being forced to do evil acts in the Overmind's name. DeMatteis's plot had hinted at an intriguing premise, namely the idea that fascism is often allowed to take hold because it presents itself in the guise of order, protection, and safety. Under the Overmind's control, president Kyle Richmond (Nighthawk) claimed he was "trying to save our nation from foreign invaders."

Mark picked up on that thin thread. As *Squadron Supreme* #1 begins, US society is in disarray, and the team is desperate to undo the damage they caused. Hyperion suggests this is an opportunity to use their powers to "abolish war and crime, eliminate poverty and hunger, establish equality among all peoples, clean up the environment, cure disease and even cure death itself." Nighthawk, wracked with guilt over his role in the takeover, balks. "What if the people will not accept the utopia you give them? Will you force them to take it?" Once the team decides to follow Hyperion's plan, Nighthawk quits, and sets about gathering a resistance force.

This becomes the central conflict of the series, and one that allows Mark to bring a real-world relevance to the story. In addition to the dangers of fascism and authoritarianism, Mark used *Squadron Supreme* to address gun control, criminal rehabilitation, political divisiveness, and the responsibility of the powerful to help the less fortunate. And within the context of addressing these political and societal concerns, Mark raised complex moral questions.

The Squadron start their project with good intentions. Resident genius Tom Thumb—who is one of the series' most sympathetic characters—invents a Behavior Modification Machine, which basically allows for localized brainwashing and the elimination of the urge for criminal behavior. Amphibian protests vehemently, saying it's unethical to meddle with free will, even if the Squadron only offers it on a voluntary basis. His misgivings are almost immediately proven justified when the Golden Archer secretly uses the B-Mod Machine to make Lady Lark—who has just refused his marriage proposal—fall madly in love with him. And yet when the Squadron uses it on Institute of Evil members Foxfire, Quagmire, Dr. Decibel, Lamprey, Shape, and Ape X, all of those characters become contributing members of the team, and some of the most noble and likable ones at that.

Mark walks this line throughout the series, demonstrating how the decisions the Squadron makes in the name of peace and prosperity seem justified, but also how in cumulation these decisions ultimately lead to very dark places. Upon encountering the series for the first time, a reader might even believe that Mark himself had not firmly chosen a side. He said, "I took pains to show the good side of everything [the Squadron] did. So that, with luck, I fooled some people for awhile into thinking it was morally acceptable or at least expedient."

But, as Macchio wrote, Nighthawk "spoke with the voice of the real Mark Gruenwald." In issue #12, when the character stands over a defeated Hyperion and says, "Your Utopian system is a failure because it requires beings as powerful and good as you to prevent its abuse. Today's utopia could be tomorrow's totalitarian state—all because you gave men the means to create it," we know exactly where Mark stands. But it's also worth noting that even Nighthawk is not fully admirable, as in his quest to stop the Squadron he makes both minor and major ethical compromises.

The back of the 1997 trade paperback collection of *Squadron Supreme* hails it as "a deconstructionist parable of the superhero paradigm in a real world setting." Couched in the typical Marvel hyperbole was the kernel of truth. While not "deconstructionist" in the literary criticism sense, the story does pull apart and examine some of the fundamental components of superhero comics. The most prominent of these is the question of why superheroes don't try to solve the problems of the world. But Mark also takes on one of the biggest challenges of mainstream superhero stories, namely that major changes in status quo typically happen at a glacial pace. Stan Lee coined the term "illusion of change" to describe the way comics teased sweeping alterations and then eventually reset them to status quo. Status quo did change in Marvel comics, but it was usually incremental and gradual—Peter Parker made his way through high school and college; Reed Richards and Sue Storm got married and started a family.

What Mark did in *Squadron Supreme* was accelerate that years-long process into a twelve-issue timeline. This had the effect of amplifying the already soap-operatic tendencies of superhero comics. In *Squadron Supreme*, characters betray one another, quit the team, get replaced by doppelgangers, form deep romantic connections, become blinded and maimed, and make no-win decisions.

And then there are all the deaths. The body count in *Squadron Supreme* is staggering, with twelve characters meeting their ends throughout the series, often in gruesome ways. But it never feels gratuitous, because each and every death is treated with gravity and met with trauma. Mark was no fan of death in comics, but he also felt that for *Squadron Supreme*'s story to land properly with readers there would have to be massive casualties. He even ended up killing more characters than he'd originally intended, including original Squadron members Blue Eagle, Golden Archer, Tom Thumb, and Nighthawk.

In this way, as Macchio put it, "Mark had found a way to make a major statement about the place of superheroes . . . and do it while indulging a deep passion for those selfsame entities." So even amidst the chaos and moral dilemmas and mayhem, Mark's love of comics still shines through brightly. This shows up largely in the way he builds the Squadron's world, hinting at a rich past, both distant (Professor Imam, Power Princess, and Blue Eagle's father were all in a Justice Society of America–like institution called the Golden Agency) and recent (the team's villains, the Scarlet Centurion, Master Menace, and the Institute of Evil all play important roles). The style and format of the book is very traditional, even down to the semi-awkward recappings of the previous issue's events. Mark also indulged in some tried-and-true comic book tropes, such the changing of identity and costume (Golden Archer, after being expelled by the team, christens himself the Black Archer and gets spiffy new duds) and the evil doppelganger (an alternate reality Hyperion, whom Mark and Ralph had written about in *Marvel-Two-In-One* #67).

Squadron Supreme has an uncanny number of things in common with DC's *Watchmen*. Alan Moore and Dave Gibbon's twelve-issue opus debuted in September 1986, the month after *Squadron Supreme*'s twelfth issue. Both featured analogue versions of another company's heroes (in *Watchmen*'s case, the characters had originated at Charlton Comics), both starred complicated and not-completely-admirable characters, both reflected the fears and anxieties of the 1980s, and both took on the question of whether or not it's okay to do something grossly unethical if you believe it's for the greater good.

Marvel and DC are notorious for copycatting each other's ideas, but this wasn't a case of that. The two series were created concurrently, with their creators having no idea what the others were doing. In a 1986 interview, Mark said he couldn't wait for *Watchmen*, and that Gibbons was "quite alarmed to see that I had inadvertently hit upon some of the same things they were going to do." Gibbons needn't have worried, as of course *Watchmen* was immediately recognized as a masterpiece and outsold *Squadron Supreme* by a large margin.

Comic creator Michael Fiffe points out that in a head-to-head battle, the odds were always stacked against *Squadron Supreme*, noting that *Watchmen* had a consistent creative team, was free of Comics Code Authority constraints, and was presented without ads in an artfully designed deluxe format. *Squadron*, on the other hand, had three different artists (original artist Bob Hall couldn't keep up with his deadlines, which necessitated having John Buscema and Paul Ryan spell him), and looked like a standard Marvel comic of the day, with blurb-filled covers, ads, and newsprint printing. But Fiffe also asserts that this makes *Squadron Supreme* all the more shocking and remarkable, because it used the "language of traditional comic booking" to tell a very nontraditional story. It was like a comic book Trojan horse.

Throughout his career, Mark aspired to create an archetypal character. He never achieved that, but with *Squadron Supreme* he created an archetypal superhero story. The plot and themes of the series have been loudly echoed by the acclaimed likes of *Kingdom Come* (1996), *The Authority* (1999), *Identity Crisis* (2004), *Civil War* (2006), *Injustice: Gods Among Us* (2013), and countless others. Comics writer Chris Roberson says that, for this reason, Mark is "the father of modern superhero comics." He argues that, though it addressed real-world concerns, the dramatic events of the *Squadron Supreme* limited series actually pushed its fictional world farther away from the reality we know. And he asserts that this has now become a common practice in superhero comics, both monthly and prestige, as well as in Marvel and DC's never-ending parade of events. Roberson writes, "The current state of superhero comics, with its obsessive attention to continuity and rationalization, line-wide crossovers, multiple realities, and increasing divergence from the real world, resembles nothing so much as a Mark Gruenwald comic writ large. . . . And the mainstream superhero comics of today resemble Gruenwald's *Squadron Supreme* more than they resemble the mainstream comics of the day."

One wonders if Mark would be flattered by this, or if he would be dismayed. The transition to more adult-oriented superheroes has brought the comics world some fantastic stories, but it has also resulted in some misguided indulgence in *Squadron Supreme*–style mayhem and moral ambiguity without any sense of pathos or ethics. There's no evidence that Mark wrote *Squadron Supreme*

Mark dedicated *Squadron Supreme: Death of a Universe* to his father, "this universe's wizard supreme." Photo circa 1987. Courtesy of Gayle Coughanour.

with the intention of creating a model for what superhero comics should be. His response to the question, "Why don't superheroes take on real world problems?" was to show what the cost of that would actually be. And it's telling that—though Mark continued to be concerned with reality and relevance in his comics—he never attempted to do anything like *Squadron Supreme* again.

Even when he returned to the Squadron characters for the 1989 graphic novel *Death of a Universe* (with Paul Ryan returning on pencils, inked by Al Williamson) he told a story that felt much more traditional and Gruenwaldian. Despite the absence of the moral conundrums that defined the limited series, *Death of a Universe* is a distinguished piece of work filled with fascinating and clever twists, including the revelation of the world-destroying threat as Thomas Lightner, the same villain from Mark and Ralph's 1980 "Pegasus Project" story.

CHAPTER 8

D.P.7 and the New Universe (1986–1989)

> It is my belief that the ultimate intent of comic fantasies should be to reconcile the fiction as much as possible with reality.
> —Mark Gruenwald, 1971

In 1985, editor-in-chief Jim Shooter sat down with Marvel CEO and president James Galton to discuss how best to celebrate the publisher's upcoming twenty-fifth anniversary. Shooter had a radical plan: A complete reset and restart of the Marvel Universe that would take every title back to its essential premise, and "weed out the glitches, bad stuff, and stupidities" that had built up over two decades. Galton, well aware that Marvel was the number one comic company and that sales were fantastic, balked at the idea of blowing it all up.

So Shooter offered up an alternative plan. They'd launch an entirely new universe, one focused on presenting superheroes in a more realistic and science-based manner. Galton went for it, and gave Shooter a generous $120,000 budget to develop and promote eight new titles to be released in 1986. But not long after getting this approval, Marvel's parent company, Cadence Industries, hit financial hardship, and the budget for the project was slashed to nothing. His dreams of luring big-name talent no longer possible, Shooter decided instead to cobble together a team of Marvel staffers—including Archie Goodwin, Tom DeFalco, and Mark Gruenwald—to see what ideas they had stored away.

The result, after some collaborative refining, was the New Universe. The creative team devised a set of guidelines that would differentiate this fictional reality from the Marvel Universe. The eight series—*Justice, Marc Hazzard: Merc, Nightmask, Psi-Force, Spitfire and the Troubleshooters, Kickers, Inc., Star Brand,* and *D.P.7.*—would take place in present-day 1986. The world would be exactly like ours: Ronald Reagan was president of the United States, *Dallas* was on TV, Lional Richie's "Dancing on the Ceiling" was on the radio. At least up to the point of the "White Event." The event—an idea Mark lifted from comics he made as a teenager—was a worldwide flash of energy on July 22, 1986, that triggered paranormal abilities in a small percentage of the Earth's population. This was to be the only fantastic element of this universe, at least to start with. There were to be no aliens, space gods, alternate dimensions, or better-than-real-world technology. Time would pass normally, so twelve issues of a New Universe title would cover one year in its characters' lives. Shooter promised that the New Universe would depict "the world outside your window."

This was all well and good in theory, but it immediately fell apart in practice. The lack of budget, the fact that most of the creators were pulling double or triple duty, and the short turnaround time meant that the New Universe lacked coherence from the start. Editorial and creative teams quit or were replaced almost immediately, some even before a single issue was published. Many of the concepts had been developed before the "rules" of the New Universe were set, and thus broke them: *Star Brand* featured an alien traveler, *Justice*'s premise was that the main character was from an alternate dimension, and the technology behind Spitfire's armored suit was better than possible at the time. Right away it wasn't the world outside your window.

The one exception was Mark's contribution: *D.P.7*. Of all the New Universe books, *D.P.7* remained most true to the parameters of the line, and was the most consistent in its execution and quality. This was due not only to how much Mark valued structure and order in his fictional realities but also to the fact that Mark had helped design the New Universe to be an ideal venue for him to work toward two of his biggest writing goals: trying new things and portraying superheroes realistically.

Originally called Missing Persons, then Displaced Paranormals, *D.P.7* got its final title at the suggestion of Jack Morelli. The book follows seven superpowered Wisconsinites who find themselves residents at the Clinic for Paranormal Research, where the management has less-than-altruistic intentions. In his typically analytical way, Mark prepared for the series by undertaking a study of fourteen superhero teams and making a list of their common elements. He then set about creating a team book that would defy all those conventions. Instead of everyone being around the same age, there would be a large range, from teen to senior citizen. Teams usually had one female member, two at most; *D.P.7* had three. As opposed to the usual all-white teams, Mark included two Black members. The team didn't have a headquarters or charter or even a common purpose most of the time. "I tried to go against type everywhere I could," Mark said in a 1986 interview.

Mark took many of the *D.P.7* character concepts from his Idea Book, and further refined them in meetings with the New Universe brain trust. Randy O'Brien creates a living shadow. Dave Landers has added an incredible amount of musculature. Stephanie Harrington has a supercharging effect on herself and others. Charlotte "Charly" Beck can make things sticky or slippery. Dennis "Scuzz" Cuzinski emits an acid-like substance. Lenore Fenzl's skin emanates a tranquilizing effect. Jeff Walters has super-speed.

These are all more-or-less typical superpowers, but Mark's innovation was in how he presented them. "We were making stories about people with super-powers," Mark wrote in 1989, "not superheroes."

The seven paranormals don't wear costumes or fight crime. They invent code names, but regularly forget to use them. And their powers are just as often portrayed as curses as they are blessings. Lenore has to cover every inch of her skin lest she drain energy from those around her, and eventually she becomes dangerously addicted to the energy she gains from using her powers. Scuzz is constantly destroying his clothing, and can't even kiss a woman without burning her lips. Jeff Walters's super speed causes him to vibrate constantly and make it so he is unable to fall asleep naturally. There's not a single main character who fully embraces their newfound power, and Mark presents a sharp contrast when orphan (and comic book fan) Evan Huebner bonds with an antibody creature that Randy rejected. Evan redesigns the antibody so he vaguely resembles Johnny Thunder's Thunderbolt, and he learns to "ride" inside it, clearly finding great joy in the experience.

This commitment to being "relentlessly realistic" about the consequences of extraordinary things extended to Mark's plotting of the series, too. Surprisingly, Mark didn't plot ahead on *D.P.7*, instead taking things one issue at a time. That doesn't mean he was careless or didn't build on and call back to what had happened before, but he did give himself the freedom to improvise. Though he loved writing *Captain America*, he was working primarily with elements that had been long established. With *D.P.7* he created the elements himself, and was able to change, adapt, and invent as he pleased. "With *D.P.7* I can do what I want," he said.

He took advantage of that in both content and form. In terms of the latter, he played with storytelling conventions. The book's pacing has more in common with episodic television than it does with typical comic book structure. Events unfold in real time, and each issue has a beginning, middle, and end. In sharp contrast to his over-the-top use of recaps in *Squadron Supreme*, Mark didn't use them at all in *D.P.7*, only flashing back to fill the reader in on events that occurred in the time jumps between issues.

The conflicts in *D.P.7* are largely internal or interpersonal. While the impetus for the action is the group being on the run from their captors at the Clinic for Paranormal Research, most of the actual drama comes from relationships and self-exploration. Mark also brings in themes such as domestic abuse, race relations, religion, AIDS, and unrequited love. None of these are treated in a heavy-handed or preachy way, but instead as realities of the world outside your window, and inside your home.

Artist Paul Ryan (paired most frequently with inker Danny Bulandi) was a huge part of *D.P.7*. His artwork always prioritized clarity of storytelling above all else, but was also finely detailed and carefully crafted, and it got better and better as the series progressed. Mark was thrilled to work with him. "Let's hear it for Paul," Mark said in a 1988 interview. "He captures all of these great moments of expression. He's really made me able to do a character-intensive book. He's also a fountainhead of ideas on where to take all of the various characters. . . . He makes my job easy." Paul, for his part, noted that the most difficult aspect of his job was "trying to condense over-plotted stories," which was a friendly jab at Mark.

Mark and Paul both put a lot of themselves into the book. In 1986, Mark revealed, "*D.P.7* is about as autobiographical as it can be in a fantasy world. The characters are all a little part of me." Paul Ryan added in a 2009 interview, "We brought many of our real-life experiences, both positive and negative, to the series." Charly's background as a dancer is a nod to Mark's time in Terpsichore. When the displaced paranormals land in New York near the end of the series, Randy takes a job as a messenger, just as Mark had in his early days in the city. His antibodies are named after some of Mark's favorite comedians: the Marx Brothers and the Three Stooges.

Mark also inserted his friends—sometimes in name, sometimes in personality—into the story. Lenore Fenzel got her name and profession directly from Mark's high school Latin teacher (the real Ms. Fenzel once called Mark's dad to tell him that she'd seen Mark and girlfriend Holly Lindsay holding hands in the hallway, something she found highly inappropriate). Stephanie, a blond former cheerleader, seems to be an analogue of Holly. Dave Landers's name is a play on David Lofvers, as are some of his personality traits; and his friend Susan was named after the real-life David's

The cover of the final issue of *D.P.7* by Paul Ryan, Danny Bulandi, and Paul Becton, 1989. Copyright Marvel Comics.

real-life wife. Charly was probably a nod to Charlie Haasl, and Steph's lunkheaded husband Chuck was likely after Roy "Chuck" Hoglund. Randy and Jeff might have gotten their names from a couple of Mark's former JLA Club compatriots, and Randy being a medical student was probably a nod to his friends Eugene Wright and J. Mark Madison, both of whom became doctors.

This likely helped Mark identify more closely with the players in his stories. Paul Ryan said, "Mark absolutely believed in the New Universe and especially the cast of D.P.7. We talked about them as if they were people we knew and cared about. We loved our characters."

There's also the fact that D.P.7 takes place in Wisconsin. Throughout the series Mark uses real cities he knew well, such as Racine, Sheboygan, Wausau, and Rhinelander. Besides being a link to his formative years, it was also another way for Mark to do something different. "Wisconsin is a very normal place," he remarked. "But it almost becomes exotic because you don't see it much in comics."

✐ ✐ ✐

The tumult of the New Universe's conception and execution was reflected in its reception and sales, and within a year Jim Shooter realized something dramatic had to be done. He decided to slash the line in half, canceling *Marc Hazzard: Merc*, *Codename: Spitfire*, *Kickers, Inc.*, and *Nightmask* and placing the four remaining books under the auspices of Mark's former assistant, editor Howard Mackie. Mackie hadn't even started work on this shake-up when there was an even bigger one: In April 1987, Shooter—having lost the confidence of the Marvel higher-ups—was removed as editor-in-chief. In the ensuing shuffle, Mark was promoted to second-in-command, which meant that he was now the overseer of the New Universe.

The changes came almost immediately. In addition to trimming the line, moving the books off the newsstands and into direct-market stores, increasing the paper quality (and the price),

Mackie brought on superstar writer/artist John Byrne to take over *Star Brand*. Mackie, Byrne, and Mark put their heads together to devise a big event to bring fresh attention to the New Universe. The result was a "prestige format" squarebound special called *The Pitt* (1987) in which Ken Connell accidentally destroys his hometown of Pittsburgh while trying to rid himself of the Star Brand power. The implications of the event were felt across the remaining New Universe titles.

Mark felt many of the other NU writers had misunderstood the premise of "the world outside your window," thinking that they couldn't do anything that would fundamentally change the world, mistaking a realistic approach for a staid one. He wrote that this led the New Universe titles to feel more like made-for-TV movies instead of the big budget special effects extravaganzas they should have been. *The Pitt* was an effort to correct that.

In addition to its consistency in quality, *D.P.7* had regularly been one of the best-selling New Universe titles. Even so, Mark and Paul were relieved to have survived the cut. And after *The Pitt*, the creative team gamely changed their approach to meet Mackie's expectation of more action in the New Universe books. The *D.P.7* characters either enlisted in the Army or were recruited by the C.I.A., which gave them an excuse to start wearing costumes (colorful, but still mostly realistic), and go on "missions." Mark and Paul incorporated all of this nearly seamlessly, and without sacrificing their focus on character development.

As was his wont, Mark also worked to "correct" some of the previous New Universe writers' transcription mistakes, and to incorporate what he saw as worthwhile elements of the canceled books into the ones that carried on. Mark, Mackie, and Byrne rewrote Star Brand's origin so that Ken Connell didn't get the power from an alien, but from his future self. Mark helped writer Peter David reset *Justice*'s premise, and brought Nightmask, Jack Magniconte (of *Kickers, Inc.*), and Jenny Swenson of *Codename: Spitfire* into *The Pitt*, in addition to its follow-up, *The Draft*.

The New Universe as a whole definitely improved with these changes, but the damage had already been done. Nothing could save the line from the general air of failure surrounding it. Readers may not have completely agreed—all of the surviving NU titles were profitable until the end—but new editor-in-chief Tom DeFalco decided to pull the plug.

D.P.7 #32 (June 1989) was the final issue of the series, its cover emblazoned with a tongue-in-cheek "#32 in a thirty-two issue limited series" banner. Having received advance notice of the cancellation, Mark and Paul were able to give their characters a proper send-off, introducing an intriguing new twist—a potential cure for paranormality—but also resolving Dave's long-standing unrequited love for Steph. Remarkably, the duo had done every single issue—plus *Kickers, Inc.* #5, which was essentially a thirty-third issue—monthly for almost three years straight. The other New Universe titles, in contrast, had an average of five different writers and eight different artists.

Not long after the end of the New Universe, Mark used two consecutive "Mark's Remarks" columns to ruminate on the line's creation and demise. In the first he praised some of the more daring conceptual elements of the line. In the second he discussed how some of those same elements hampered its commercial potential. In addition to mentioning some of the creative chaos behind the books, Mark also wondered if creating a second universe unwittingly set up a competition: "Asking readers to love two universes may have been too much to ask," he wrote. In terms of *D.P.7*, he self-critically posited that, in trying to avoid team book cliches, he got too far away from why people buy team books, and superhero comics in general.

That may have been true in terms of sales, but by approaching the book the way he did, Mark ended up turning *D.P.7* into a meditation on what exactly makes superhero comics *creatively* successful. The answer was not just the powers and fantastical concepts, nor only the big themes they explore, nor solely the personalities of the characters themselves, but the combination of all of those things all in service of one another. Mark would later admit that writing the book had helped him overcome his reputation as someone who was "more concerned with reconciling ancient discrepancies than with telling whopping good yarns." It showed both his fellow professionals and his fans that he was capable of much more than continuity and corrections.

CHAPTER 9

Captain America (1985–1995)

> Here is a man who does not just accept responsibility for himself, but for the society that has fostered him—a man who realizes that he is a symbol to his fellow man, and constantly strives to be worthy of that trust.
>
> —Mark Gruenwald, June 1985

When Mark took over as writer of *Captain America* in summer 1985, he had three main goals. First was to give the character and the title a sense of consistency and stability it had rarely had; following Stan Lee's departure from the book, no writer had stayed longer than three years. Second was to increase sales. The book was among the lowest sellers of the original 1960s Marvel characters and had been considered for cancellation. Mark's third goal was to make the character relevant to the rapidly-changing times. Mark felt that the concept of Captain America lent itself naturally to an exploration of topical matters. This was a character, after all, whose very first appearance found him socking Adolf Hitler in the jaw. In a letter printed all the way back in *Captain America* #181 (January 1975), Mark praised writer Steve Englehart for incorporating "the political trauma of Watergate" into the book.

So along with streamlining and remaking the title's status quo—which included shuffling around the cast and having Cap establish a national hotline—Mark devised stories that would reflect the big issues facing the United States in the 1980s. The early 1980s had seen a swell of patriotism, as well as a successful effort by Republicans to position themselves as the only true patriots. This was fueled by an extremely popular president, Ronald Reagan, and his hardline stance toward the USSR.

This new patriotism was personified by Sylvester Stallone's John Rambo (in 1985's *First Blood, Part II*) and Arnold Schwarzenegger's John Matrix (in 1985's *Commando*), who mercilessly mowed down foreign enemies. On TV (and in toy shops) *G.I. Joe: A Real American Hero* portrayed the United States military as a force of unambiguous good against a terroristic organization called Cobra. Not-so-incidentally, Mark called the *G.I. Joe* series Marvel published starting in 1982 "the most highly influential comic of the '80s."

Captain America—a World War II veteran who made the ultimate sacrifice and then returned to continue to fight for his country—should have seen a rise in popularity during this time, but his clean-cut, follow-the-rules persona seemed antiquated. It would have been both canny and prescient to have Captain America become a jingoistic, no-mercy sort of crimefighter, and to lean fully into the conservative politics that were popular at the time. But to Mark that would have been a betrayal of the character. He felt that Captain America should embody the American Dream, "the belief that common folk from anywhere on Earth can come to a land of opportunity where they are free of forces that oppress them because of race, color, or creed ... to realize their aspirations and fullest potential."

Mark's personal politics were very similar to those of his parents. They were staunch Democrats, believing strongly in the ideal of government and political office as vehicles for promoting the greater good (Myron was an avowed letter-to-the-editor enthusiast, and he used the forum to argue in favor of taxes for public services, the worth of public education, and the value of embracing a multicultural viewpoint). But Mark wanted to elevate Cap above politics. In 1987 he said, "Judging by the mail, I think fans have a lot of erroneous assumptions about Captain America's personal beliefs. They somehow think he should be a conservative Republican despite the fact that he assumed his position during

FDR's Democratic era. Cap is truly non-partisan, not liberal or conservative. He represents the entire country and its people."

So Mark's mission was to thread the needle of remaining true to Captain America's character while also acknowledging the zeitgeist. On a surface level he adopted some of *G.I. Joe*'s tricks, not only in the parallels between the Serpent Society and Cobra, but also in the use of what Mark called "paramilitary hardware." One could have made a robust toy line out of the various vehicles Mark introduced to help Cap get around, including a van, motorcycle, the Flagship (a jet with the shield symbol on each wing), and the Skycycle.

On a deeper level, Mark used his Cap stories to explore the complexities of trying to abide by an ethical and moral code in a time when the definition of those concepts was a matter of debate. To do this, he created a large slate of new antagonists, each of which in some way represented an ideological challenge to the American dream and to Steve Rogers's values and principles. In his very first issue, Mark introduced the garish Madcap, who sows anarchy and spouts nonsense. Mark said Madcap represented young people who believe that "life has no meaning, nothing makes sense, everything is a joke, and nothing is worth taking seriously."

In subsequent issues Mark created villains that represented antinationalism (Flag-Smasher), vigilantism (Scourge), fear of nuclear war (Overrider), steroid abuse (Power Broker), domestic terrorism and the moral majority (the Watchdogs), and environmental extremism (Brother Nature). Whereas Captain America's enemies had once tended to come from other countries, these were all homegrown. And despite all having noble intentions—world peace, protection of the planet's natural resources, heath and wellness, the elimination of crime—these antagonists' methods are misguided and frequently violent. As Cap tells Brother Nature in #336 (December 1987), "That's the danger of crossing the line and becoming a renegade. There's no telling how far you may be obliged to go to accomplish your ends. You might even end up harming that which you most want to protect."

This approach served the dual purpose of giving depth and relevance to Mark's stories, while also defining Steve Rogers's moral fortitude. During the initial Flag-Smasher story (#321, September 1986), Cap is forced to shoot down one of the villain's ULTIMATUM goons to stop him from opening fire on a crowd of people. It's a decision most ethicists would support, but Cap is wracked with guilt over having to take a life. This story, accompanied by a Mike Zeck cover featuring Captain America grimly firing an Uzi, was a direct message to readers who wanted Cap to become more like Rambo.

Captain America #321 was the best-selling issue of Mark's tenure up to that point, likely due to the misleading image on the cover. That tension between giving the fans what they thought they wanted while actually delivering a completely different message led directly to the biggest challenge that Mark created for Steve Rogers: John Walker, a character initially known as the Super-Patriot. When he's first introduced, Walker is a showboating braggart who has been physically augmented by the Power Broker. He issues a public challenge to Steve Rogers, whom he says is out-of-touch and no longer up to the job of representing the United States. Walker's definition of what it means to be an American patriot is that you talk big and profit big from being a part of the most powerful nation in the world. Walker has three costumed buddies who call themselves the Bold Urban Commandos, the "BUC-ies" for short, a clever reference to Steve Rogers's original partner Bucky Barnes. In issue #327 (March 1987), they set fire to an international student house on the University of Wisconsin–Madison campus in the name of antiterrorism. "Roughin' up a bunch of un-American slimeballs sure does my patriotic heart good," one of them remarks.

This display of violent xenophobia might have been enough to make readers truly appreciate the inherent goodness in Captain America's character, and to communicate what the character stood for in terms of patriotism, but Mark took it further. In what would become the defining story of his time on *Captain America*, his next step was to have John Walker take over the Captain America name, costume, and shield.

This comes about when the US government stakes a claim on the Captain America concept, and tells Steve that he can only continue in the identity if he agrees to become their agent. Reasoning that working directly for the Reagan administration would undermine his ability to transcend politics, Steve gives up being Cap. The government then installs John Walker as Captain America, with former BUC-ie Lamar Hoskins as his sidekick, Battlestar (Mark originally called the character Bucky, but assistant editor and writer Dwyane McDuffie, a Black man, pointed out that calling a Black character Bucky had racist connotations and Mark quickly agreed to make a change). Things go okay at first, but soon Walker's moral failings and violent tendencies get the better of him. The most shocking of these is when he brutally murders Professor Power. Through John Walker, Mark gave readers a Captain America who abides by a twisted definition of patriotism, showing blind loyalty to the government without any ethical considerations.

While these story developments flowed quite naturally from everything Mark had been doing from the beginning, that was mostly a matter of luck. Mark hadn't initially planned for John Walker to take over the mantle of Captain America. That idea came along with a somewhat more cynical purpose behind it, namely super-charging the book's sales. He claimed that a writer had three "cheap tricks" they could use to shake things up: a costume change, a death, or a replacement of the title character. Mark had done the first and the third. And sure enough, sales skyrocketed and the media took notice, with Mark doing interviews with National Public Radio and the *Washington Post Magazine*.

By giving readers what they thought they wanted—a violent, conservative Captain America—Mark proved his point. Most of the book's fans despised John Walker. "I never got such hate mail in my life," Mark said. Readers also predicted Walker would die. That would have allowed Mark to complete the trifecta of cheap tricks, but instead he became determined to defy reader expectations. Despite himself, Mark had developed an affection for Walker as the storyline progressed, which is no surprise considering deeply flawed characters populate his writing. Indeed, after returning Steve to his rightful place as Cap, Mark would refashion Walker as the US Agent, and find a place for him on the West Coast Avengers. He'd revisit the character a few times, most notably in a 1993 miniseries.

On the topic of flawed characters, after "The Captain" storyline, pink-haired Serpent Society member Rachel Leighton, codenamed Diamondback, gradually becomes a partner for Cap and a love interest for Steve. Her inclusion in the book would become one of the standout elements of Mark's run on *Captain America*. Diamondback is a criminal with a tragic past, and pairing her with Cap allowed Mark another opportunity to explore the benefits and the limitations of Steve's moral code. He inspires Rachel to make many positive changes in her life, and in turn she helps Cap to become less rigid. For instance, in issues #380–382, when she asks for his help in bringing down the Serpent Society, she also requests that he spares her friends Asp and Black Mamba from punishment. Cap says that would be wrong, and an angry Rachel goes off on her own. When Cap eventually does help, he allows Asp and Black Mamba to remain free after all.

In addition to revealing new dimensions to Cap's character, Diamondback goes on a character journey of her own. Over Mark's run Rachel transforms from a throwaway background character to one that's fully defined and sympathetic. She endures several trials and triumphs, emerging stronger, more well-rounded, and more independent.

In the last two-thirds of Mark's run, *Captain America* became less overtly topical, though there were some exceptions. Red Skull, who had returned in #350, was reimagined as a businessman. As author Jason Olsen wrote of Mark's Red Skull, "The more modern version does not flaunt his Nazi ideology, but he hides it with Capitalistic attire and flourishes." Businessmen and corporations were the go-to villain archetype in the late 1980s and 1990s. In the "Streets of Poison" storyline, Mark and artist Ron Lim took on the drug epidemic, while also examining a reader question that piqued Mark's interest: If the Super Soldier Serum is a drug, isn't Captain America the embodiment of better living through drug use? In issue #385 (July 1991), Mark and artist Rik Levins brought back the Watchdogs with the twist that Cap's friend Mike Farrel is one of the group's newest members, again demonstrating just how readily strong moral convictions can become extremism.

Mark continued to explore and reaffirm the relevance of Captain America himself. While this could be seen as repetitive, in the context of the times it was necessary. Though the shift toward violent, morally ambiguous antiheroes had begun in the late 1980s, it really took hold in the early 1990s when the comics industry was flooded with highly armed protagonists for whom ethics were not a consideration. So Mark forced himself—and the character—to ask the question of whether or not it was time for Cap to retire. In issue #383 (March 1991), the fiftieth anniversary issue, one of the Elders of the Universe sends Cap on a journey through American myths and legends—including John Henry, Paul Bunyan, and Uncle Sam—in order to get him to agree to retire and ascend into their ranks. But Cap resists. "I'd rather be a living hero," he responds, "than an inactive legend."

Nearly all of Mark's stories from 1991–1995 represent some sort of challenge to Cap's resolve, be they twisted-mirror versions of himself (Americop), ethical dilemmas (whether or not to kill the Supreme Intelligence in "Operation Galactic Storm"), or enemies who were his physical superior (Crossbones). In each case, Cap reaffirms his determination to fight for his ideals.

For Mark, Captain America was an aspirational figure, and writing him was an exercise in finding the very best in himself. In a 1990 "Mark's Remarks" he wrote, "Writing a character as virtuous as Captain America is a real stretch for a regular fella with a mixed

Cap demonstrates his resolve in *Captain America* #383, 1991. Art by Ron Lim, Danny Bulandi, and Steve Buccellato. Copyright Marvel Comics.

bag of failings and personality flaws like I have. Cap's value system is far more idealistic than mine could ever be."

It had been a difficult task to constantly inhabit that mindset, but in the end Mark was the perfect writer to usher Captain America through one of the roughest patches in superhero comics history. His ability to communicate the extraordinary decency and the unflinching moral strength of the character, while also acknowledging the times in which the stories were happening, allowed Captain America to survive the late 1980s and early 1990s with his integrity fully intact, and put him in prime position for a resurgence in popularity.

CHAPTER 10

Mark the Executive Editor (1987–1993)

> Consistency is not a straitjacket—it's a rocketpack! One that may be a bear to master, but when you get the hang of it, it enables you to go higher and farther than you would otherwise have been able.
> —Mark Gruenwald, January 1992

When Jim Shooter was dismissed as Marvel's editor-in-chief in April 1987, the board offered the job to Tom DeFalco. DeFalco urged Mark to take it instead, but Mark didn't want to be editor-in-chief because "the boss has to be the mean one." So DeFalco took the job, and made Mark his second-in-command.

In nearly ten years at Marvel, Mark had proven to have a unique ability to navigate both office politics and creative egos, and in the executive editor position he found a job perfectly suited to those skills. He had a diverse range of duties, including working with editors on project development, standing in as chief when DeFalco was gone, running editorial meetings, conducting classes for assistant editors, compiling the Bullpen Bulletins page, coordinating crossovers between characters from different editorial teams, and helping maintain line-wide consistency.

Of the many roles Mark played as executive editor, the one he relished most was serving as "prime custodian" of the overarching narrative of the Marvel Universe, a place in which, he once asserted, had more stories set in it "than in any other fictional reality ever devised by any human being." Though it likely wasn't in his official job description, Mark used his power and his breadth of knowledge about Marvel history to "patrol the corridors of the Marvel Universe, keeping track of things, preventing my fellow creatives from damaging our common universal backstory by heinous acts of commission or omission."

In concrete terms this meant coordinating between editorial teams on crossovers and character appearances, as well as cross-referencing character names and power sets to avoid duplication. He took some of the rules he'd used as a writer and made them official Marvel policy. In regard to characters, he felt that there was no reason to create a new character when a preexisting one could serve the same purpose. "Sometimes," he wrote, "it takes more creativity NOT to create a character." Though Mark invented a fair share of heroes and villains himself, his writing and editing career is more distinguished by his refurbishing of older, underutilized ones (including Mockingbird, Squadron Supreme, and Quasar).

Mark also reached back to his work on the *Treatise on Reality in Comic Literature* and *Omniverse* to devise a set of ten rules for time travel in the Marvel Universe. The main feature of Mark's system was the concept of time travel resulting not in alterations to the present or future, but in the creation of divergent timelines. True to form, Mark didn't invent these rules out of whole cloth, but instead based them on established Marvel history. His own fan letter to *Marvel Team-Up* #49 (September 1976) had pointed out that interdimensional time travel had been established in *Fantastic Four* #152 (November 1974).

Mark became well known as the company's resident "Continuity Cop" or "Minister of Continuity in Marvel Comics" (MC Squared), but he didn't like the word "continuity." He felt it was too often misinterpreted as "a slavish single-minded devotion to trivial details found in ancient storylines and a strange compulsion to resurrect and glorify said details at the expense of other story values." He preferred the term "consistency" instead, as that indicated a commitment to making all the details work together. In a 1993 "Mark's Remarks," he admitted this was a dramatic shift from his feelings as a fan and assistant editor, when, he wrote, he "reveled in obscure trivia, granting greater importance to the details than I did to the entertainment experience."

This mindset was replaced with a more pragmatic one. The man who had spent much of his early Marvel work on bringing connections, corrections, and closures to older stories wrote, "I'm more interested in making the present interesting than making the past make sense." He had also learned to accept that minor inconsistencies were unavoidable, and chose to put his time and effort into preventing the major ones, properly maintaining the sandbox so it would never need "wholesale implosion" akin to what DC did with 1985's *Crisis on Infinite Earths*.

As executive editor, Mark also made a triumphant return to the convention circuit. Starting with the 1987 San Diego Comic Con, Mark decided to make the Q&A panel "Marvel Madmen Cut Loose" live up to its name. He teamed with Ralph Macchio to shake things up. They introduced the "Orange of Inquisition"—an orange picked up from the breakfast table—to throw at audience members who wanted to ask a question. They also paused between every couple of questions to perform "Stupid Editor Tricks," such as leading an audience singalong or building a Marvel Madmen Human Pyramid out of staff members. The audience loved it, and Mark claimed that this reawakened the "avant garde exhibitionist" in him.

Through the second half of the 1980s and into the early 1990s, conventions became the primary outlet for Mark's penchant for performance. During these years, the Q&A panel morphed into a zany variety show that included skits, improv, contests, exhibitions, interviews, and plenty of audience participation, with Mark often playing the role of emcee. It was, in many ways, a return to his Cheap Laffs days. The "Marvel Madmen" panel traveled with its own backdrop and sound system, and featured activities such as the Silver Sable Wrap (with aluminum foil), butt races, freestyle raps using character names (Quasar, Ka-Zar, and the Living Laser, for example), and bobbing for comics.

Mark joked that these exhibitions "brought the dignity of Marvel's crack editorial crew to a new all-time low and the enjoyment of the attendees to an all-time high." Mark credited Tom DeFalco for participating and setting a tone for these events, but it was really an extension of Mark's unofficial role as Marvel's staff cheerleader and social director. He did the same for company picnics (in 1993, he participated in a dunk tank with DeFalco and Marvel president Terry Stewart), holidays (he organized the annual staff Halloween party), and company retreats (he led the group in games of Walleyball).

Another of Mark's passion projects as executive editor was a weekly class for Marvel's fourteen-some assistant editors, which Mark began coteaching with Tom DeFalco circa 1988. The goal was to facilitate discussions about the theory and practice of the craft of creating comic books the Marvel way, something Mark would have "paid [his] eyeteeth" for when he first started. Eventually Mark created an entire syllabus, with topics including the importance of character flaws, how to do a good letters page, balloon placement, the value of bad ideas, cover design, and the difference between a story that's complex and one that's complicated.

Mark started each class with a "media shower," in which everyone shared what TV, movies, and books they'd consumed recently, and what they'd learned about storytelling from them. He introduced unusual activities, such as having the group create a definition of heroism or invent comic book jargon. Mark welcomed dissent and argument, and often offered up his own work—both as editor and designer—for critique. "I've always taken criticism well," Mark said, "which is good 'cause I get a lot of it."

It wasn't just editors and assistant editors that Mark shared his wisdom and experiences with. He also shared it with the fans that read Marvel's in-house promotional magazine, *Marvel Age*. In addition to running the "New Talent Department," where he offered frank appraisals to aspiring writers and artists, he also continued "Mark's Remarks." Every month, from 1989 through 1994, Mark published a new essay, each one accompanied by a caricature of him by a different artist. In these pieces, Mark waxed both philosophical and introspective. He dished on the inner workings of the

Mark's office at Marvel, 1992. The only other piece of furniture in the room was a school chair and desk for Sara. Courtesy of Eliot R. Brown.

company, explored Marvel history, dispensed advice, and guided readers through his creative process. He regarded these essays as the work of a "frustrated educator," writing "I get a certain pleasure out of explaining things, imparting information, and sharing ideas about subjects I know and like." Mark's conversational tone and willingness to open up made readers feel as if he was someone they knew.

A recurring topic—and one that related directly to the New Talent Department—was breaking into the comics industry. Having been on both sides of the submission process, Mark had strong opinions about the way people approached seeking work at Marvel. Some hopefuls didn't appreciate Mark's suggestion that they not start with the company that has "the highest possible standards of what constitutes professional quality" or that being "arrogant, disrespectful, or unpleasant" wasn't going to serve them well. At the heart of Mark's message to would-be creators was the same approach he took: "I truly believe that those 'destined' to toil in the fields of professional comics will find a way to do so no matter what obstacles the uncaring, unfeeling, insensitive powers-that-be may throw in their paths."

In addition to traveling around the country to attend conventions, the executive editor position afforded Mark unique experiences. He attended the Buchmesse, the Frankfurt Book Fair in Germany, two years in a row, and fans lined up to meet him; it was, he reported, the first time he felt like a genuine comics superstar. In 1988 he served on the guidelines revision committee for the Comics Code Authority. And in 1992 he went with a group of Marvel editors to George Lucas's Skywalker Ranch in Marin County, California, which then housed Industrial Light and Magic. The group got a tour and gave a short presentation. For his part, Mark talked about his role at the company ("I keep track of things"), and the unique elements of the Marvel universe ("You could make a movie about any one of these things—we got 'em all!").

Being executive editor was also lucrative. In addition to his not-insubstantial freelance pay, Mark's salary ballooned, and he was able to afford a big apartment in Manhattan, and, eventually, a second home in Pawling, New York, not far from the western border of Connecticut.

Mark's ascent to second-in-command at Marvel coincided with the decline of his relationship with Belinda. There were several factors that led to the end of the marriage, not the least of which was Mark's punishing work schedule. Even in 1986, before taking the executive editor position, Mark told an interviewer he was considering going freelance full-time in order to have more time with his family. Instead, he had taken on more responsibility.

Mark and Belinda's divorce was finalized in 1988. Three-year-old Sara remained in her mother's custody, but visited Mark on Wednesdays and every other weekend. By all accounts Mark was an enthusiastic and devoted father, drawing upon his own active inner child. Not surprisingly, he most relished being creative with Sara, telling her long, involved bedtime stories (sometimes with a sly, personalized moral), inventing a fantastical origin story behind a bracelet, teaching her Morse code in case of an alien invasion, or making up jokes while putting together a model of Pinhead from the 1987 film *Hellraiser* ("Who is Pinhead's favorite female singing group? The Pointer Sisters"). When she was a little older, Mark kept a small desk in his office just for Sara, with colored pencils and paper for her to draw with. Mark wanted Sara to learn which rules were important and which ones should be broken, and he wanted her to be brave and confident. "Girls can do anything," he'd tell her.

Mark took his divorce hard, but eventually he started seeing someone new, Jan Greenbaum. They were a great match, but after about a year and a half into their relationship, Jan was diagnosed with melanoma. Mark faithfully stuck by Jan as the cancer spread and killed her. He was devastated by her death. Roy Hoglund recalls meeting up with Mark in Oshkosh around this time and finding his old friend uncharacteristically pessimistic and cynical.

Mark threw himself into work and parenting, and was eventually able to regain his sense of hope. In late 1990 he made a pact with Ralph Macchio that they would both meet someone in 1991. Sure enough, in January 1991, Mark met Catherine Schuller, a model who had come to the Marvel offices to audition to play She-Hulk in personal appearances. She didn't get the job, but Mark got her phone number.

A Pittsburgh native, Catherine studied psychology, music, and drama at Chatham College. She moved to New York in 1974—just a year after Mark had—and started carving out a place for herself as a cheerleader (for the New York Cosmos), stand-up comedian, and actress. In the early eighties she cofounded a comedy troupe called The Nerve! for which she wrote, performed, directed, and designed. The troupe led to other opportunities for Catherine, including gigs writing industrial films and brief interest from *Saturday Night Live*, but the most significant was a backstage visit from a modeling scout. By the time she met Mark, Catherine was a prominent figure in the plus-size fashion world, working for the prestigious Ford Modeling Agency.

In Catherine, Mark found someone who could match his boundless energy and restless creativity. "It was like turning on a light," Roy says of Mark's turnaround. "He now had a partner in crime." Catherine knew nothing about comic books, but she sat down

Mark and Catherine with flower girl Sara at their wedding, October 1992. Courtesy of Catherine Schuller.

and read every single thing Mark had written. She also embraced the aspects of comics fandom that connected with her own experiences and passions. She began to accompany Mark to conventions, becoming an early adopter of cosplay, and using her improv background to join in the Marvel Madmen mayhem.

Mark and Catherine were married on October 12, 1992. The K-Otics played at the reception, and the couple's first dance was to "One More Kiss, Dear," the old-timey tune sung by Don Percival in 1982's *Blade Runner*. The reception also included what Mark called a "21 Bun Salute" in which all of the guests feted Mark and Catherine by sitting on whoopee cushions in unison. Mark and Catherine celebrated by attending a distributors convention in Puerto Rico, and then heading for St. John's for their honeymoon.

CHAPTER 11

Quasar (1989–1994)

> But for the most part, what motivates me is a little bit off the beaten track—I can't help it. Evidence for my peculiar aesthetics can be found in my choice of writing assignments... I really love the mid-to-low popularity characters I'm doing.
> —Mark Gruenwald, 1993

Those who write and speak about Mark's legacy tend to justifiably focus on the groundbreaking *Squadron Supreme* or the record-setting *Captain America*, but his heart, soul, and essence was in *Quasar*. In every single way, Mark's fifty-nine-issue, five-year run on *Quasar* is his most personal work. This was where Mark most thoroughly explored his childhood fascination with DC Comics, and was where he most clearly expressed his beliefs, interests, and proclivities.

Mark had long held affection for the character originally known as Marvel Man, who had made just four appearances before Mark and Ralph Macchio claimed him for "The Pegasus Project" in *Marvel Two-In-One*. There the writers gave the character a new job (as Project Pegasus's security chief), a perfunctory origin (his researcher father uses him to test Marvel Boy's quantum bands), and a civilian identity (Wendell Elvis Vaughn). It was around this time that Mark began collecting ideas for a Quasar series.

In the meantime he brought Quasar along on other projects. In *Marvel Team-Up* #113 (January 1982), Mark paired Quasar with Spider-Man, portraying them as an oil-and-water combination who manage to defeat the Lightmaster together in spite of their anathema for one another. Mark also used Quasar in *Marvel Team-Up Annual* #5 (November 1982), and gave the character an entry in the *Official Handbook of the Marvel Universe*.

In 1984, Mark pitched a series featuring Quasar and Ransak the Reject, a character from Jack Kirby's *Eternals* series. But *Squadron Supreme* was approved first, and then his gigs on *Captain America* and *D.P.7* consumed all of Mark's freelance time. When it became clear that *D.P.7* and the New Universe were doomed, and that Marvel would be looking to add new titles to fill the void, Mark reworked and resubmitted his *Quasar* proposal. This time, thanks in part to his promotion to executive editor, the project got a green light.

Mark knew a book featuring a mostly unknown and unproven character would face an uphill battle for sales, so in an attempt to make *Quasar* a better bet, Mark used his editorial power to have the character join the Avengers. In a back-up done with artist Mark Bagley in *Avengers Annual* #18, Mark established that Quasar's quantum bands make him "Protector of the Universe" (and thus a successor to the 1970s hero Captain Marvel), showcased his powers, and pitted Captain America and Hawkeye in an argument over which Avengers team got to have him (Cap won). Quasar is portrayed as competent and powerful, but wet behind the ears, and deeply insecure about the level of responsibility he's been given.

The initial creative team for the book was the same as it had been for *D.P.7*, with Paul Ryan, Danny Bulandi, Paul Becton, Janice Chiang, and editor Howard Mackie all continuing on. *Quasar* debuted in October 1989. Because it had been five years since the character's last appearance, and because Quasar had never received a proper origin story, Mark used the first couple of issues to address both of those things. From there he established a simple premise that would carry the book through its first two years: Eon, a cosmic entity who protects all life in the Marvel Universe, has foreseen their own assassination. As Eon's chosen champion, Quasar must investigate and prevent this prophecy from coming true.

Quasar would be the first series to explore the cosmic side of the Marvel Universe from the perspective of a human protagonist. Of all the different genres and genre mash-ups represented in superhero comics, it was cosmic stories—ones that deal with "forces and phenomena on a grand scale"—that most engaged Mark's sense of wonder as a young reader. It went all the way back to his early obsession with Gardner Fox's *Justice League of America*, and this is the first way in which *Quasar* served to capture Mark's essence. The book, especially in its first year and a half, is a tribute to the types of stories Fox wrote about the JLA, Adam Strange, Green Lantern, and the Flash. This is evident in the "alien-of-the-month" format of the early *Quasar* issues, and in the character's tendency to expound upon the scientific principles behind his powers (DC's Silver Age comics often incorporated educational facts in the stories). The book even briefly included a letters-page feature elucidating concepts such as hyperspace and the electromagnetic spectrum.

Mark's most Fox-indebted story was *Quasar* #17 (December 1990), featuring a race between Earth's fastest inhabitants, and a not-so-subtle cameo from a then-dead Barry Allen (the Flash). The issue also cemented the Eternal Makkari as a partner for Quasar, mirroring the frequent pairing of Green Lantern and the Flash. Even when he wasn't making overt references to it, Mark had a tendency to draw on elements of Gardner Fox's approach and philosophy, including his use of vocabulary and thought bubbles, his tendency to have characters cleverly think their way out of trouble, and his devotion to craftsmanship, research, and humanism.

In many ways, Mark shaped Quasar into his on-the-page stand-in. Wendell Vaughn grew up in Oshkosh, Wisconsin, in a house on Westhaven Drive. He has a younger sister named Gayle, and a father who's a teacher. He plays guitar, has a Captain America poster on his childhood bedroom wall, and even sometimes uses his quantum bands to manifest nunchucks, a weapon Mark practiced regularly, and was known to demonstrate at conventions.

Mark, his sister Gayle, and brother-in-law Wendell model their Alternity T-shirts, 1977. Courtesy of Gayle Coughanour.

Mark saw it as his role to protect the Marvel Universe, so he gave Quasar the same job.

Other details from Mark's life were remixed in Quasar's life. Wendell's name comes from Mark's then brother-in-law, Wendell O'Connell. His secretary Kayla got her name from Mark's niece (Gayle and Wendell's oldest daughter). Later, Ereshkigal arrives in the form of Holly Steckley, so called after Mark's high school girlfriend, Holly Lindsay.

The parallels between Mark and Quasar become undeniable in "The Bearable Lightness of Being" from *Quasar* #18 (January 1991). In this self-contained issue, Wendell finds himself visiting Oshkosh without any memory of his life as a superhero. The story, drawn by Greg Capullo, is full of Gruenwald easter eggs, from referring to the University of Wisconsin–Oshkosh as "UW-Zero" to a comic-filled clubhouse above the garage to two sly cameos by

Augmento to the appearance of Origin (a character Mark invented in *Personal Entropy* in 1977) to a neighbor named Norma, after Mark's mother. Even the structure and tone of the story—which involves Quasar becoming involved in a struggle between two abstract entities, Origin and the Unbeing—is a tribute to Mark's beloved *Twilight Zone*.

Mark didn't just bequeath Wendell the surface details of his life, he also gave him his preoccupations and beliefs, especially as they related to the emotional lows Mark experienced in the late 1980s. Quasar as a series is inordinately concerned with death, and not in the multiple-characters-meet-their-end way of *Squadron Supreme*, but in a facing-your-own-mortality and exploring-what's-next way. Right away in issue #2, Wendell fights off "existential angst" in the personified form of the black-clad Deathurge. Quasar "dies" twice in the course of the series, and finds his way back both times. His father dies, and so does Eon, but not before asexually reproducing to create their own successor, Epoch. In addition to Deathurge (who appears multiple times throughout the series), there's even the Harvey Comics–inspired Kid Reaper, who serves as Wendell's personal avatar of Death (and this doubles as a reference to Mark's childhood love of Caspar the Friendly Ghost).

Quasar #49 (August 1993) features a more grounded depiction of the specter of death, when Wendell returns to Earth to discover that his mother has been diagnosed with breast cancer. This sends him on a frantic—but fruitless—search across the universe for a cure. In the end Lisa Vaughn has a successful mastectomy and is declared cancer-free. It was almost as if Mark were trying to write a happy ending for Jan, who had not survived her own cancer. It's difficult not to think of this when Quasar ruminates, "it's as if a curtain's been dropped and I can now see the world the way it really is—a cold dark place, inhospitable to thinking, feeling lifeforms."

Since death hung so heavily over *Quasar*, religion naturally came up as well. Though he had grown up attending the congregational church and served as a youth minister, by young adulthood Mark no longer identified himself as a Christian. Both *Augmento* and

Concept Radio Theatre explored the dangers of religious fanaticism taken too far. Mark would continue that in his professional career, subtly in *Squadron Supreme* and *Captain America*, and more overtly in *D.P.7*, which featured a storyline in which a cult called the "White Eventists" who believe it's their job to help bring about the end of the world.

In *Quasar* Mark focuses less on the dangers of religion and more on the futility of it. Wendell is a firm nonbeliever, and says as much multiple times throughout the series. At his father's funeral he says, "When you die, the bundle of energy that was you dissipates—returns to the world, there's nothing left of you anywhere" (#21), which is not far from Mark's own quip in *Marvel Age* #100 (May 1991): "I have no problem believing in the afterlife, it's the afterdeath I'm not so sure about." And when Wendell says he's no fan of "religious rigamarole" (#35), it puts into context Mark's directive in his will forbidding the words "God," "Jesus Christ," and "Heaven" from being used in connection with his funeral and/or memorial service.

Spiritually, Mark was very much at home in the Marvel Universe, a place where gods from every culture take actual physical form. Mark wrote that this created a paradox in which "everybody's notion of god is right and true, [but] no god (or belief system) is true to the exclusion of all others." He was a member of both the Skeptics Society—an organization that champions a rational and critical approach especially toward matters of science—and the American Humanist Association, which promotes the tenet that "you can be good without a belief in god."

Quasar also serves as a guided tour of Mark's work history, revisiting the characters and concepts he had edited, written, and/or drawn, and bringing the various strands of his work together into one place. Fittingly, considering that's where he first wrote the character of Quasar, Mark drew heavily on his *Marvel Two-In-One* stories from ten years earlier, reviving—and further developing—characters such Her, Moondragon, Aquarian, and Maelstrom. Mark also used *Quasar* to return to the Squadron Supreme, with

Quasar #13 picking up exactly where the 1989 *Death of a Universe* graphic novel left off and incorporating the Squadron as semi-regular cast members.

Perhaps the most shocking way in which Mark mined his past in *Quasar* was his choice to revisit D.P.7 and the New Universe. It began *Quasar* #31 (February 1992), the continuation of a story in which Quasar must track down versions of the Living Laser from various realities. Initially, Mark wanted to have Quasar accidentally travel into the Omniverse to Mighty Mouse's universe, but the cartoon rodent's Marvel comic had just been canceled. So Mark and artist Greg Capullo instead had Wendell become trapped in the New Universe. There, he meets D.P.7, and ends up using the Star Brand to return home.

But it didn't end there. Mark would use this issue as the basis for the major plotlines of the rest of the series. At the end of *Quasar* #31, Mark has Quasar bring one of Randy O'Brien's Antibodies and the Star Brand into the Marvel Universe. This would eventually lead to the entire New Universe being incorporated into the Marvel Universe, though with travel between the two still impossible. It was a huge change of heart for Mark, who said in a 1986 interview that he'd fight to the end any attempt at a MU/NU crossover. In a humorous piece in *Marvel Age* #131 (December 1993), Mark explained that he felt it was inevitable that someone would revisit the New Universe, so he decided to do it preemptively, his way.

Quasar was also a forum for Mark to indulge in his love of creating connections, corrections, and conclusions. In terms of connections, Mark's affection for *The Eternals* shines through, from his use of speedster Makkari as Quasar's sidekick to instances where he connects backstory elements for characters such as Hyperion, the Overmind, the Stranger, and Maelstrom to the Eternals and Deviants. The most significant of these was Mark's choice to tie the origin of the original Marvel Boy (Robert Grayson) and the quantum bands to the Eternal Uranian colony established in the *What If...* back-up stories Mark wrote in 1980.

In response to letter writer K. S. Jessie in *Quasar* #51, Mike Rockwitz wrote, "It's no one's duty to wrap up old loose ends from discontinued series; it is however one of our writer's perverse pleasures." Just as he had with Omega the Unknown and Nova before, Mark used Quasar to bring closure to previous projects. Perhaps the most left-field of these was his choice to bring back the Chief Examiner and the Black Fleet from *Questprobe*. Mark had drawn the first issue of what was supposed to be a twelve-issue series, but only three comics (and three accompanying computer games) were released before Adventure International went bankrupt and left the story unfinished. For several issues of *Quasar*, Mark conducted a running subplot in which Kayla and Holly get caught in the middle of the battle. The aftermath of that plotline then became a central element of the *Starblast* crossover, showcasing Mark's knack for using old stories to generate new storytelling opportunities.

✏ ✏ ✏

Though it would end up lasting for five years, concluding in July 1994 with issue #60, *Quasar* teetered on the brink of cancellation for most of its run. Despite consistently good artists (Paul Ryan was succeeded by Mike Manley, Greg Capullo, Andy Smith, and John Heebink), and various attempts to gain a wider audience (crossovers such as "Operation Galactic Storm" and *Infinity War*; guest stars like Ghost Rider and Punisher), the book couldn't survive the midnineties comics slump.

The failure of *Quasar* to catch on was not a surprise. In many ways its underdog status was baked into the concept. There's the fact that Mark was doing what amounted to a Silver Age DC tribute comic in the grim-'n'-gritty early 1990s, and there's the fact that the character of Quasar himself—insecure, self-serious, too kindhearted and gentle to be chosen as a S.H.I.E.L.D. field agent—was a

The final page of the final issue of *Quasar*, 1994. Art by John Heebink, Aaron McClellan, and Paul Becton. Copyright Marvel Comics.

square peg in round-hole times. In this way, writing *Quasar* was an act of oppositional defiance. Mark followed his muse and poured himself into the book without regard for trends or popularity, something writer Michael Fiffe summarized as "creative tenacity in the face of lukewarm reception."

This made both Mark and the character easy targets. *Wizard*—a magazine that served as an industry tastemaker in the nineties—called Quasar "one of the crappiest characters in existence" and labeled the comic "lame-o." Mark also endured plenty of negative reviews from *The Comics Journal* and *Comic Buyer's Guide*, not just for *Quasar* but for nearly everything he wrote. This anti-Mark faction was summarized by letter writer Patrick C. Duke in *Quasar* #45, who alleged Mark's writing was characterized by "corny dialogue, ridiculous situations, out-of-character guest stars, and a planet full of misfit 70s one-shot characters."

Mark took criticism well, but to have his most personal work lambasted so brutally was surely disheartening. At the same time, it was fitting because failure was a recurring theme in *Quasar*. Like Wendell, Mark took his work deadly seriously and had a tendency to beat himself up over his shortcomings, both real and perceived. The series's final issue finds Wendell despondent over losing Kayla, and deciding to leave Earth. On the last page, he flies away into space. John Heebink draws Quasar in a heroic pose, but with his face twisted in anguish. He monologues in thought bubbles, first explaining how he faked his death, then bidding farewell. His final words double as a message from Mark: "Please, everyone. Be well . . . and don't think badly of me. I didn't succeed in everything I set out to do, but I tried my best. What more could I do?"

CHAPTER 12

Death and Afterdeath (1995–present)

> I believe many things are worth the effort of doing and doing right, even though ultimately what difference it will make is nil. In the time I have allotted me, I must find a way to carve out a significant life.
> —Mark Gruenwald, 1989

For Mark, 1995 was characterized by failure and setbacks. Personally, he faced a spate of difficulties small and large, including the death of his grandfather Eddie, and his parents' declining health. Professionally, his editorial stewardship of Marvel had faltered in fundamental ways and his writing career had stalled.

With *Quasar* canceled in the summer of 1994, Mark's only ongoing book was *Captain America*. Within the year that was gone, too. Mark didn't want to leave the book—he had more stories to tell—but a combination of factors spelled the end. During Mark's ten years on the book, *Captain America* had never been a bestseller, but it had remained profitable, with consistent sales throughout the late eighties and early nineties. Starting in late 1994 and early 1995, *Captain America*'s circulation fell lower than it had been when Mark took over in 1985. Management decided to replace Mark with writer Mark Waid. In public, Mark blamed his departure on the fact that he had recently taken over editing the traditional superhero line, which included *Captain America*. He claimed to not be comfortable with being his own editor-in-chief: "All writers need editors . . . who have enough teeth to be able to say, 'If you don't do such and such, you're off!'" Privately, though, he made it clear to those close to him that he'd been forcibly removed. He took it very hard.

Much as his last issues of *Quasar* did, Mark's final *Captain America* stories reflect his personal mindset. Here, Cap learns that the super-soldier serum in his body is deteriorating and begins wearing an exoskeleton armor that accelerates his condition with each use. In Mark's final issue on the title (#443, September 1995), done with artist Dave Hoover, Cap learns he only has twenty-four hours to live. Instead of reflecting on his many accomplishments, he ruminates on his failures. "I've stopped evildoers of all kinds over the years," he thinks, "but I wonder have I even once inspired any evildoer to forsake evil? I doubt it." He visits Crossbones in prison, hoping to find some shred of hope of redemption, but the villain only laughs at him. He goes to see Ram, the teenager who helped run his hotline, and learns that the boy's mother has been severely injured in a carjacking. This only reinforces his feelings of inadequacy. Though there are plenty of characters whom Cap inspired to take a better path in life—Hawkeye, John Walker, Diamondback, D-Man—he doesn't give a thought to any of them. Steve Rogers, in Mark's mind, was someone who is never satisfied: There's always more that could have been done, and there's always more to do. Clearly Mark felt this himself. He had helmed *Captain America* longer than any other writer by a wide margin, writing the book for ten years and 137 issues, but still felt he hadn't done enough.

On the editorial side, what Marvel's marketing department dubbed as a "Marvelution" felt like a bloodbath to Mark. During Mark and Tom DeFalco's tenure, Marvel's sales and profitability were higher than they'd ever been. But the company had also gone through several changes that would ultimately make Marvel unrecognizable from the publisher Mark had joined in 1978. It had been sold twice, became a publicly traded company, and grew rapidly by acquiring other companies and dramatically increasing its publishing output.

In 1993, after an extended period of record-setting sales and growth, the comic book industry went bust. Two-thirds of comic book shops closed and several upstart comics companies went belly-up. According to DeFalco, Marvel weathered the bust fine, and every title the publisher was putting out in 1994 was profitable. But Marvel's executives were nervous about the state of the industry, and made panicked moves, including buying competitor Malibu Comics, and acquiring their own distributor, Heroes World. Regarding the latter, DeFalco told the executives that it was "the stupidest idea I've ever heard," one of many opinions that led to him stepping down as editor-in-chief in November 1994.

Mark was in line to succeed his boss and friend, but that didn't happen. Rather than designate a single replacement, the powers-that-be decided to split Marvel into five groups, each with its own "editor-in-chief." Mark was put in charge of the mainstream superhero titles, including *Captain America, Avengers, Thor,* and *Fantastic Four*. Though the job title made it sound like Mark had finally ascended to the top spot at Marvel, the job was effectively a demotion; Mark had gone from overseeing the entire Marvel Universe to being in charge of a fraction of it. The cohesive universe Mark had tended so meticulously was now divided into factions, with intertitle consistency only an afterthought.

Initially Mark continued to play the role of Marvel's most enthusiastic and devoted cheerleader. In a June 1995 Bullpen Bulletins column, he wrote, "Marvel is retooling itself to give you, the readers, better stuff than ever before in state-of-the-art packaging." The next month he praised Marvel's purchase of Heroes World, a move that would ultimately prove disastrous. In the office, Mark did what he could to try to boost morale. "The worse it got," editor and colorist Kevin Somers recalled, "the more he showed up with enthusiasm and kept trying to cheer people up."

But the reality was grim. The five-way split of the editor-in-chief job fractured the cohesive universe Mark had worked so hard to safeguard. And a 40 percent reduction in titles meant a severe cut to personnel. Mark witnessed fellow staffers, some who'd been at Marvel as long he had, shown the door with little ceremony. And as editor-in-chief of the Marvel Universe line, he had to fire creative teams on canceled books, including four editors, an act he called "the single worst thing I've had to do in my 18-year career at Marvel."

✏️ ✏️ ✏️

After about a year of Marvelution, the company abandoned the five-way editorial split, and appointed Bob Harras as the singular editor-in-chief. Harras had been in charge of the *X-Men* titles, the most popular and best-selling of all the Marvel books. The decision to hire him reportedly was made with heavy input from Jim Lee and Rob Liefeld, who had both left the company in 1992 to form Image Comics but were in negotiations to take over four Marvel books, all from Mark's stable of titles. Mark's final issue as editor-in-chief was *Fantastic Four* #409 (February 1996). He reverted to his executive editor title, working on projects such as a Top Cow/Marvel crossover.

Previously, when things were challenging at the editor level, Mark could take solace in the creativity of his freelance work, but even that stream had dried up. After *Quasar*'s cancellation, his initial plan had been to write an ongoing team book starring Quasar, Silver Surfer, and Beta Ray Bill—*Star Masters*—but the failure of *Starblast* put that on hold. When the title did appear in December 1995, it was in the form of a three-issue miniseries that concluded in a different title not written by Mark, a set of circumstances that were emblematic both of Mark's loss of cachet and of the chaos at the company during this time.

Early 1996 found Mark planning a return to Squadron Supreme, and completing a handful of journeyman-type projects: A one-and-done Dr. Strange story, a mini-comic detailing the origin of the Combos snacks brand mascot *Combo Man*, and a Spider-Woman back-up tale with artist Pat Broderick in *Sensational Spider-Man Annual '96* that brought Mark's professional comics career full circle. Mark seemed to feel that, though he was only forty-two years old, his heyday had passed. In a 1995 Bullpen Bulletins he wrote,

"Nobody stays on top forever. But being a has been is generally preferable to being a never was. No one listens to never wases, but has beens can still make for good copy on occasion. I ought to know, eh?"

It was becoming more and more difficult for Mark to keep up a veneer of optimism at work. He became uncharacteristically withdrawn, and started seriously considering his exit options. In a 1987 "Mark's Remarks" he had written, "If your hobby becomes your profession, you better find another hobby." But it seems now he had decided that he'd better find another profession altogether. Always a big cinema buff, he had started taking screenwriting classes. He was also working on manuscripts for a couple of children's books, and was entertaining the notion of writing a sci-fi novel. He was so disillusioned with comics that he didn't immediately jump at an offer from Mike Carlin—who had left to work for DC in 1986—to switch companies.

It's ironic, then, that a final high point for Mark was working with Carlin to spearhead 1996's *DC vs. Marvel Comics*. The four-issue story was the first large scale crossover between the two publishers, and featured an innovative online vote that allowed readers to decide who would win various face-offs between characters.

Mark didn't write the series, but he and Carlin were heavily involved editorially, creatively, and promotionally. The book made national news, which gave Mark and Mike a chance to play up the long-standing rivalry between Marvel and DC. The follow-up was even more audacious, a series of one-shots under the banner Amalgam Comics, featuring mash-ups of characters from each company such as Dark Klaw (Batman and Wolverine) and Super-Soldier (Superman and Captain America). Mark and Mike were instrumental in bringing these combined concepts to life, and mashed themselves up into editor-in-chief "M. M. Carwald" for the "Amalgam Nation" page in the one-shots. All of this led Mark to say, "I've been a comics fan for twice as long as I've been a comics editor, and in no previous series I've worked on have I felt the sensibilities of my professional and fannish sides so completely engaged."

In early August 1996, still pondering his future, Mark headed north with Catherine and Sara to Pawling for a week's vacation. Wendell, Gayle, and his nieces and nephew—Kayla, Brenna, and Aaron—were coming for their yearly visit, and Mark had a week of fun and activities planned. As a respite from the stress of work, Mark had thrown himself into transforming the seven-acre, forest-ensconced Pawling property into a private wonderland. He built a wall out of large rocks. He constructed a treehouse for Sara, as well as a playground with parallel bars, a climbing tower, rings, and a teeter-totter. He was also working on a second treehouse for himself, this one with an escape hatch and a fireman's pole. He gave the trees names from mythology (such as Daedalus and Yggdrasil), punningly dubbed a giant boulder "Ragnarok," and named various other landmarks in honor of friends who came to visit.

The house itself was midcentury modern style, with a bright, sunken living room that hung over a ravine. Just as he had in the house on Westhaven, Mark claimed a room that served as his creative workshop, not just for writing, but for painting, and customizing action figures (of which Mark was an obsessive collector), and other projects.

On the first night of Gayle's family's visit, they ate ice cream, played frisbee, and talked about their plans for the week. Sometime in the early morning of August 12, Mark suffered a massive heart attack in his sleep. Catherine woke to his choking expulsions of air. Terrified, she began screaming his name. Gayle rushed in, along with twelve-year-old Kayla, who had just completed a class in CPR, to guide her in resuscitation. Someone called an ambulance. Mark was technically alive when the ambulance arrived to take him away, but he was already gone.

Mark believed a person should know exactly how many days they'd been alive. He'd made it to 15,761.

Mark and his in-progress treehouse in Pawling, circa 1994. Courtesy of Gayle Coughanour.

As the news of Mark's death spread to his many friends and coworkers, the most common reaction was that it was his most elaborate prank yet. Mark—who exercised regularly (jogging, mostly), ate well (he once wrote would eat within his own subphylum but not any closer than that, meaning birds and fish, but no cows or pigs), rarely drank alcohol, didn't smoke or do drugs, and survived the most dangerous physical stunts unscathed—couldn't possibly have had a heart attack.

As it turns out, Mark had coronary artery atherosclerosis, plaque build-up in his arteries. Mark wasn't aware of this, but there was at least one warning sign: David Lofvers recalls that Mark had been complaining of feeling uncharacteristically tired in the weeks before his death, attributing it to a cold or the flu. Many of his friends and family speculate that the stress of his professional life combined with the strain of his physical labor at the Pawling property were just too much for his heart to take.

Homages and tributes poured in immediately. In his announcement of the news to the Marvel staff, president Terry Stewart

Stan Lee makes a cameo in this photo of Mark and Catherine, 1992. Courtesy of Catherine Schuller.

wrote: "It can be said without reservation that Mark embodied the spirit of what we like to think Marvel is and should be." All comics cover-dated December 1996 featured a one-page "In Memoriam" highlighting Mark's contributions to Marvel both on the page and off, and effusive tributes from a host of professionals, including Stan Lee, who wrote, "Even in a field populated by so many highly competent and highly talented individuals, Mark Gruenwald was truly outstanding. We have lost a most valued member of the comic book firmament, a firmament whose stars can shine a bit brighter for Mark having been among us."

Mark's onetime assistant editor Mike Carlin told *Wizard* magazine, "The greatest thing about working with Mark Gruenwald was the sheer joy he got from comics, and the excitement he was able to communicate in his work, both writing and editing." Walt Simonson said, "Mark was a perfect combination of fan and professional. He could write and he could edit, and he brought a fan's enthusiasm and breadth of knowledge about comics to his work."

Mark's former mentor Dennis O'Neil wrote a moving remembrance for *Wizard* that was as much about the person as it was the professional. "The capacity for locating the joyous made Mark a happy man, one of the few I've ever known. It wasn't that life had been particularly kind to him . . . but in the grim hours, he found some alchemy of courage and optimism and refused to pity himself." O'Neil also mentioned Mark's love of teaching other professionals about the "building, care, and maintenance of fictional universes."

Tom DeFalco's initial comments also focused on Mark the teacher. Writing of the assistant editor classes, he stated, "I can't believe that anyone has had a greater impact on the next generation of comic book professionals than Mark." Evidence plays that out. Many of the editors Mark taught in those classes have gone on to become prominent in comics and elsewhere, including James Felder (who uses Mark's course syllabus as a writing professor at NYU) and Lysa Hawkins (senior editor at Valiant). And there are dozens more who weren't in Mark's classes, but still count him as a key figure in their career journey, including writers Paul Cornell (for whom reading *Omniverse* was a formative experience) and Fred Van Lente (who at age fifteen received an *Avengers* script and an encouraging letter from Mark).

Small memorial services were held in both Oshkosh (at the Seefeld Funeral Chapel) and in New York City (at the Eliot Library Ethical Cultural Center). In September 1996, Catherine organized a larger celebration of Mark's life at the New York Film Center, dubbed "Gruenycon I" by writer Peter David. Speakers included Walt Simonson, Tom DeFalco, Paul Levitz, Dennis O'Neil, and Mike Carlin, all of whom shared memories of Mark's irrepressible joie de vivre.

There was a Mark memorabilia museum curated by David Lofvers from his own collection, including displays of Mark's early work, envelope art, video letters, and a photo gallery. There were also presentations of *Cheap Laffs* highlights, and a memorial video Catherine had put together by her friend Sally Jessy Raphael's editing team. The video began with a clip from the *Twilight Zone* episode "The Incredible World of Horace Ford," about a toymaker who's obsessed with his childhood. From there it went into highlights from Marvel Madmen panels and Mark and Catherine's wedding before ending with an extended montage of photos from childhood on. Unsurprisingly, many of the photos featured Mark wearing some sort of costume. The evening ended with a reprise of the "21-Bun Salute," featuring twenty-one Marvel staffers sitting on whoopee cushions simultaneously.

These celebratory memorial events became a semi-regular occurrence in the ensuing years, starting with a Mark-focused panel at the 1997 San Diego Comic-Con that ended with 200 attendees exiting the room in a *Monty Python*–style silly walk. Gatherings in 2007 (at the Museum of Comic and Cartoon Art) and 2016 (at Space Ibiza New York) each followed a similar structure to the original event, uniting a host of Marvel staffers former and current to share Mark stories.

✏ ✏ ✏

Mark's work shows a consistent fascination with death and its accompanying mysteries and absurdities, so it's no surprise that he chose to stage one last act of humorously macabre spectacle. Mark stipulated in his will that all of his organs be donated to science, his body cremated, and that the cremains be "mixed with printer's ink when a comic book is being printed."

Catherine connected with Bob Harras and Marvel's Production Liaison Alison Gil. Gil, who, thanks to the early nineties cover gimmick craze, was used to unusual comic printing requests, arranged for Mark's ashes to be sprinkled on the black plate for a poster by Claudio Castellini featuring a group shot of approximately fifty Marvel heroes and villains. Catherine traveled to Eastern Color Printing in Avon, Connecticut, to oversee the process herself.

But it didn't stop there. Next, Catherine and Marvel decided to use the cremains to print a collection of the 1985 *Squadron Supreme* miniseries. Catherine stirred the ashes into the ink herself, picking out chunks of bone as she went. Released in 1997, the initial print

Mark poses in the in-progress coffin he was building for his upcoming Halloween party, June 1996. Copyright and courtesy of David Lofvers.

run of 5,000 copies of *Squadron Supreme* gave readers a little part of Mark, both literally and figuratively.

The story of the comic creator who loved comic books so much he wanted to become one was so bizarre it made national news, and would end up being included in multiple weird-but-true type books such as *Ripley's Believe It or Not*. In 2011 the Investigation Discovery channel show *The Will: Outrageous Final Wishes* featured a segment about Mark and his ashes. Catherine, who was initially incredulous about Mark's request, has now embraced it. Her latest project is putting Mark's "Ash-o-graph" (a resin stamp of Mark's signature dipped in ink and his ashes) on copies of a new edition of *Contest of Champions*. It's just another example of how Catherine has wholeheartedly embraced her role as the torch-bearer of Mark's legacy, and constantly dreams up innovative ways to keep Mark's spirit alive for his fans. She also regularly hosts Gruenwald-centric panels at various conventions, and has teamed with Daniel Hort to create CosMODA, which marries fashion design and cosplay with runway modeling. During the 2022 New York Fashion Week, the CosMODA event featured the likes of Captain America and Quasar, as well as members of the Squadron Supreme and the Serpent Society.

✒ ✒ ✒

Mark's hometown of Oshkosh, Wisconsin, has honored him in many ways. The day after Mark's passing, his friend Roy Hoglund—who had become a professor at the University of Wisconsin-Oshkosh—got in touch with the university's foundation with an idea to establish a memorial scholarship in Mark's name. The result was the Mark Gruenwald Arts Foundation Fund, a $1,000 tuition award for a sophomore or junior who is involved in at least two areas of the arts. The latter stipulation was Roy's idea, to honor the way Mark rarely limited the forum or format of his creative expressions. The scholarship was promoted in Mark's December 1996 tribute page, and had $20,000 in donations within a month, supercharged by a $10,000 contribution from the Comics Magazine Association of America.

Another stipulation of Mark's will was that the Oshkosh Public Library receive bound volumes of his work, and so in 1997 Catherine arranged for that, as well as a dedication ceremony that included a small exhibit of Mark memorabilia and featured the unveiling of the color version of the poster printed with Mark's ashes, a framed copy of which is displayed in the library's children's section.

Myron and Norma Gruenwald were able to attend and see their son honored, but neither lasted long after his death. Norma succumbed to multiple myeloma in December 1997. Myron died of a heart attack six weeks later. Surely Mark would never have achieved what he did without the incredibly generous support they gave him. In 1977 Norma wrote of her son, "His natural exuberance, zany wit, and zest for living always give us a little extra lift."

Catherine and Sara with a portrait of Mark by Bolivian-born artist David Banegas, 2018. The painting now hangs in the Oshkosh Public Library. Courtesy of Catherine Schuller.

In 2019, Oshkosh mayor Lori Palmeri declared September 28 to be Mark Gruenwald Day. This coincided with the awards presentation for the first Mark Gruenwald Comic Book Creation Challenge. The annual contest—which has multiple age categories for aspiring comic book creators—is a joint venture between the Winnebago County Literacy Council and Oshkosh businesses ZaRoni's Pizza and House of Heroes Comics and Games. After it opened in 1995, Mark became a regular visitor to House of Heroes on his trips back home, engaging in long conversations with fellow shoppers.

◊ ◊ ◊

In a 1993 "Mark's Remarks," Mark wrote about that year's unprecedented glut of superhero comics, declaring that when the readers had chosen, "Marvel will be one of the publishers left standing to fight another day." From today's perspective, that looks like an easy prediction to make, but at the time it was a statement of faith. Just four months after Mark's death, Marvel declared bankruptcy.

They slowly rebuilt, with a return to the traditional storytelling and close continuity Mark had always championed. And though his trip to Skywalker Ranch had convinced him of the unlimited potential of special effects in films, Mark couldn't possibly have guessed how thoroughly Marvel would come to dominate cinema and pop culture.

Mark's ideas have played an important part in that ubiquity, and in many ways the unprecedented level of connection and continuity between the books and the films and television shows of the the Marvel Cinematic Universe is the ultimate tribute to him. 2019's *Avengers: Endgame* and the 2021 Disney Plus series *Loki* based their depiction of time travel and divergent timelines on Mark's time travel rules. In fact, the Time Variance Authority character played by Owen Wilson in *Loki*, Mobius M. Mobius, was based on Mark (Walter Simonson created the TVA and Mobius during his 1990–1991 run on *Fantastic Four* to poke gentle fun at his former *Thor* editor's time travel rules).

Shang-Chi and the Legend of the Ten Rings (2021) not only used the battle arena idea from *Captain America* #412 but also his and Ralph Macchio's introduction of the realm of Ta-Lo in *Thor* #301. *Doctor Strange in the Multiverse of Madness* (2022) connected Wanda Maximoff to Wundagore Mountain, just as Mark and Steven Grant had in "The Yesterday Quest." The most significant use of Mark's work so far has been in the Disney Plus series *The Falcon and the Winter Soldier* (2019), which borrowed from "The Captain" storyline to introduce the Flag-Smasher, Battlestar, and John Walker.

Captain America has also become the A-list character Mark always thought he should be. Sara Gruenwald—who has inherited her father's creative polymorphism—believes this was vindication for her father's approach to Cap: "Back when he was writing, I imagined that my dad worried about Cap's future—more specifically, Cap's age-old battle of staying relevant in an increasingly modern world . . . so he would be ecstatic to know that mainstream culture backs him up 100 percent."

Mark has made his own steady ascension to legendary status, with the perception of his work steadily improving year after year, a fact cemented in July 2022 when Mark was one of six automatic inductees to the Will Eisner Comic Awards Hall of Fame. The Eisners, as they're known, have been awarded since 1988, and are widely regarded as Oscars of the comics industry. Catherine accepted on Mark's behalf.

Epilogue

MARK GRUENWALD

Adapted from *The Official Handbook of the Marvel Universe Deluxe Edition* #4 (March 1985)

Mark and his cat Demelza at his home desk in his apartment on West 70th Street, 1992. Courtesy of Catherine Schuller.

Real Name: Mark Eugene Gruenwald
Occupation: Writer; editor; artist
Identity: Publicly known
Legal status: Citizen of the United States with no criminal record
Former aliases: The Gru, Gruney, Mobius M. Mobius; Master Alternity; Patron Saint of Marveldom; King of Continuity; Minister of Continuity at Marvel Comics (MC Squared); Mr. Marvel
Place of birth: Oshkosh, Wisconsin
Marital Status: Married

Known relatives: Catherine (wife), Sara (daughter), Belinda (wife, div.), Myron (father—dec.), Norma (mother—dec.), Gayle (sister), Nanda (cat—dec.), Townshend (cat—dec.), Demelza (cat—dec.)

Group affiliation: Former member of the Boy Scouts of America, Philip K. Dick Society, Three Stooges Fan Club, the Planetary Society, The Skeptics Society, American Humanist Association, the Quaker Hill Civic Association, and the American Film Institute

Base of operations: New York City, NY; Pawling, NY

First appearance: *Spider-Woman* (volume 1) #9

Final Appearance: *Sensational Spider-Man Annual* '96

Origin: June 18, 1953

Height: 5' 9"

Weight: 150 lbs.

Eyes: Brown

Hair: Brown

Strength level: Mark Gruenwald possessed the normal human strength of a man of his age, height, and weight who engaged in moderate regular exercise.

Known superhuman powers: None.

Abilities: Mark Gruenwald could play rhythm guitar (a second level adept on a five-level scale), ride a bicycle backwards, and type for up to five hours with a cat on his lap without taking a break. He could embody two seemingly conflicting ideas simultaneously, including being a "functionally optimistic" pessimist, an innovative traditionalist, and a master of fictional reality.

Number of comics written: 385

Number of comics edited: 670 (approximate)

Number of comics drawn: 10

Number of "Mark's Remarks" essays written: 170 (approximate)

Number of Marvel Characters created: 100 (approximate)

ACKNOWLEDGMENTS

I'm grateful to work with Lisa McMurtray, Frederick Luis Aldama, and the whole team at University Press of Mississippi.

Much appreciation to those who shared their memories of Mark: Eliot R. Brown, Randy R. Domer, Gayle Coughanor, Roy Hoglund, Ken Gale, Holly Lindsay, Dean Mullaney, Aaron O'Connell, and John Wilburn.

Thanks to Bobby Hamilton for his great aid in providing research materials. Extra special thanks to David Lofvers, who generously dug into his massive Mark Gruenwald archive, and whose contributions made the book richer and more accurate.

Finally, my gratitude to Catherine Schuller Gruenwald for being so gracious and helpful through the entire research process, and for so enthusiastically carrying on Mark's legacy.

NOTES

CHAPTER 1. ORIGIN (1953-1971)

5   "exciting my imagination": Bergin, Mary. "'Augmento' creator edits comics." *The Oshkosh Northwestern.* October 27, 1979.

7   "like nothing else": Gruenwald, Mark. "Mark's Remarks." *Avengers* #282 (August 1987 New York: Marvel Comics.

7   "ruled tablet pages": Gruenwald, Mark. "Mark's Remark's." *Marvel Age* #71 (February 1989). New York: Marvel Comics.

9   "danger and excitement": Gruenwald, Mark. "Mark's Remark's." *Marvel Age* #71 (February 1989). New York: Marvel Comics.

10   "hustle and bustle": Ebert, Karl. "'It was a vision.'" *The Oshkosh Northwestern.* November 23, 1997.

11   "our contributions": Gruenwald, Mark. "Set Standards High." *The Oshkosh Northwestern.* November 4, 1967.

11   "superior work": "Superior History Work Awarded by D.A.R." *The Oshkosh Northwestern.* June 13, 1967.

11   "coffee shop": Hoglund, Roy. Interview with Paul V. Allen. December 1, 2021.

11   "scoffs and put-ons": "Underground forum for ideas." *The Sunday Times* (Oshkosh). November 9, 1969.

11   "great ad-libber": Olsen, Jim. "Backstage at 'The Will.'" *The Oshkosh Northwestern.* March 11, 1970.

12   "in the genre": Gruenwald, Mark. "A Novel Concept." *Personal Entropy* #1 (December 1976). Alternity Enterprises.

CHAPTER 2. COLLEGE YEARS (1972-1976)

15   "college Augie": Gruenwald, Mark. "Augmento" (Episode 15). *Advance-Titan.* May 15, 1975.

15   "stay together": Lindsay, Holly. Interview with Paul V. Allen. December 5, 2021.

16   "someone else's observations": Gruenwald, Mark. "Mark's Remarks." *West Coast Avengers* #24 (September 1987). New York: Marvel Comics.

16	"through movement": Amend, Patte. "Terpsichore: poetry in motion." *Advance-Titan*. September 26, 1974.
17	"science fiction radio": Ray, Steve. "Concept Radio Theatre." *Advance-Titan*. February 27, 1975.
17	"same time": Hoglund, Roy. Interview with Paul V. Allen. December 1, 2021.
18	"in there": Hoglund, Roy. Interview with Paul V. Allen. December 1, 2021.
20	"professional comic booker": Gruenwald, Mark. "Augmento" (epilog). *Advance-Titan*. December 11, 1975.
20	"at a glance": Bergin, Mary. "'Augmento' creator edits comics." *The Oshkosh Northwestern*. October 27, 1979.
21	"down-to-earth foes": Gruenwald, Mark. Letter to the editor. *Wonder Woman* #181 (April 1969). DC Comics: New York.
21	"somewhat seedy": Gruenwald, Mark. "Mark's Remarks." *Marvel Age* #99 (April 1991). New York: Marvel Comics.
22	"really mattered": Gruenwald Mark. *Captain America* #428 (June 1994). New York: Marvel Comics.
22	"for the comics": Gruenwald, Mark. "Mark's Remarks." *Iron Man* #210 (September 1986). New York: Marvel Comics.
22	"my favorite subject": Gruenwald, Mark. "Fanzy Colors." *Personal Entropy* #1 (December 1976). Alternity Enterprises.
23	"have super-powers": Gruenwald, Mark. *The Complete Justice League of America Reader*. 1973.
23	"moral or message": Gruenwald, Mark. *The Complete Justice League of America Reader*. 1973.
26	"its characters": Gruenwald, Mark. *Personal Entropy* #1 (December 1976). Alternity Enterprises.
26	"its conventions": Gruenwald, Mark. *Personal Entropy* #1 (December 1976). Alternity Enterprises.

CHAPTER 3. INTO THE OMNIVERSE (1976-1978)

27	"worlds' cosmologies": Gruenwald, Mark. "Mark's Remarks." *Marvel Age* #138 (July 1994). New York: Marvel Comics.
27	"motivated enough": Gruenwald, Mark. "Mark's Remarks." *Solo Avengers* #2 (January 1988).
28	"it was exhilarating": Wilburn, John. Interview with Paul V. Allen. June 20, 2022.
29	"one's conscience": Gruenwald, Mark. *A Treatise on Reality in Comic Literature*. 1976. Alternity Enterprises.
31	"reality-based zines": Mark Gruenwald to David Lofvers. March 6, 1977.
33	"meant to me": Gruenwald, Mark. "Mark's Remarks." *Avengers* #282 (August 1987).

33	"challenged my own": Gruenwald, Mark. "Of Omniversal Concern." *Omniverse* #1 (Fall 1977).
36	"stepping on me": Zimmerman, Dwight Jon. "Mark Gruenwald." *David Anthony Kraft's Comics Interview* #54 (March 1988).
37	"part creative": Jim Shooter—"Writer/Editors, Part 1." Jim Shooter.com, August 8, 2011. http://jimshooter.com/2011/08/writereditors-part-1.html/.
37	"publisher's face": Jim Shooter—"Writer/Editors, Part 1." Jim Shooter.com, August 8, 2011. http://jimshooter.com/2011/08/writereditors-part-1.html/.
37	"his assistant": Harrold, Jess. "Making a Mark on Cap." *Captain America 75th Anniversary Magazine* (June 2018).

CHAPTER 4. WRITER AND ARTIST (1978-1984)

38	"I've jotted down": Bergin, Mary. "'Augmento' creator edits comics." *The Oshkosh Northwestern*. October 27, 1979.
39	"into that comic": Salicrup, Jim. "The Fred Hembeck Show—Episode 72." *A Site Called Fred*. http://asitecalledfred.com/2006/09/14/the-fred-hembeck-show-episode-72-the-mark-gruenwald-show/.
42	"peripheral characters": Gruenwald, Mark. *Avengers* #192 (February 1980). New York: Marvel Comics.
44	"look him up": Lindsay, Holly. Interview with Paul V. Allen. December 5, 2021.
44	"Drawing pictures": Glass, Belinda. *Personal Entropy* #12 (circa 1977).
46	"and dramatics": Gruenwald, Mark. "The Creation of a New Limited Series: Hawkeye." *Marvel Age* #6 (September 1983). New York: Marvel Comics.
47	"bizarre appeal": Gruenwald, Mark. "Introduction." *Hawkeye*. New York: Marvel Comics. 1988.
47	"two characters": Gruenwald, Mark. "Mark's Remarks." *Marvel Age* #133 (February 1994). New York: Marvel Comics.
48	"ruin it myself": Schmitz, Barbara A. "Man's love of art, writing leads to comic book career." *The Oshkosh Northwestern*. August 17, 1986.

CHAPTER 5. MARK THE EDITOR (1982-1987)

49	"the comic biz": Gruenwald, Mark. "Mark's Remarks." *Marvel Age* #125 (June 1993). New York: Marvel Comics.
49	"quintessential": Gruenwald, Mark. "Editorial Notes." *Marvel Age* #1 (April 1983). New York: Marvel Comics.
50	"top creative periods": Gruenwald, Mark. "Editorial Notes." *Marvel Age* #1 (April 1983). New York: Marvel Comics.
51	"background details": Gruenwald, Mark. "Mark's Remarks." *Iron Man* #217 (April 1987). New York: Marvel Comics.

52 "shielded me": Valenti, Kristi. "A Denny O'Neil and Matt Fraction Conversation." *The Comics Journal* #300 (November 2009). https://www.tcj.com/a-denny-oneil-and-matt-fraction-conversation/.
52 "always wins": Gruenwald, Mark. "Mark's Remarks." *Avengers* #280 (June 1987). New York: Marvel Comics.
53 "specific comments": Gruenwald, Mark. "Mark's Remarks." *West Coast Avengers* #11 (August 1986). New York: Marvel Comics.
54 "into reality": Howe, Sean. *Marvel Comics: The Untold Story.* New York: Harper. 2012.
54 "Management": Brown, Eliot R. "Mark Gruenwald A Remembrance—Part 1." www.eliotbrown.com. Circa 2017. https://www.eliotrbrown.com/wp/mark-gruenwald-a-remembrance/. Accessed July 30, 2021.
54 "he made it": O'Neil, Denny. "In Memoriam: Mark Gruenwald (1953–1996)." *Wizard, the Comics Magazine* #65 (January 1997).
54 "close to spooky": O'Neil, Denny. "In Memoriam: Mark Gruenwald (1953–1996)." *Wizard, the Comics Magazine* #65 (January 1997).
54 "too juvenile": David, Peter. "Gruenycon." *Comic Buyer's Guide* #1194 (October 4, 1996). https://www.peterdavid.net/2012/02/10/gruenycon/.
55 "more annoying": Gruenwald, Mark. "Mark's Remarks." *Marvel Age* #100 (May 1991). New York: Marvel Comics.
58 "poorly executed": Gruenwald, Mark. "Mark's Remarks." *Marvel Age* #99 (April 1991). New York: Marvel Comics.
59 "writing the book": Harrold, Jess. "Making a Mark on Cap." *Captain America 75th Anniversary Magazine* (June 2018). New York: Marvel Comics.
59 "burned-out editor": Gruenwald, Mark. "Mark's Remarks." *Iron Man* #219 (June 1987). New York: Marvel Comics.
59 "any other": Gruenwald, Mark. "Mark's Remarks." *Avengers* #286 (December 1987). New York: Marvel Comics.

CHAPTER 6. THE OFFICIAL HANDBOOK OF THE MARVEL UNIVERSE (1983-1993)

60 "care a lot": Zimmerman, Dwight Jon. "The Marvel Age Interview: Mark Gruenwald." *Marvel Age* #56 (November 1987).
60 "too much time": Brown, Eliot R. "Mark Gruenwald Remembered!—Part 4." www.eliotbrown.com. Circa 2017. https://www.eliotrbrown.com/wp/mark-gruenwald-remember-part-4/. Accessed July 30, 2021.
61 "done someday": Gruenwald, Mark. "What Fankind Needs." *Woweekazowie* #4 (Fall/Winter 1978).
63 "no showers": Brown, Eliot R. "Mark Gruenwald Remembered!—Part 4." www.eliotbrown.com. Circa 2017. https://www.eliotrbrown.com/wp/mark-gruenwald-remember-part-4/. Accessed July 30, 2021.

64   "facts and figures": Gruenwald, Mark. *The Official Handbook of the Marvel Universe* #1 (January 1983). New York: Marvel Comics.

64   "limit the unknown": Gruenwald, Mark. "Imaginary Limits" (editorial). *The Official Handbook of the Marvel Universe Deluxe Edition* #10 (September 1986). New York: Marvel Comics.

64   "errors in translation": Gruenwald, Mark. "Veracity Quotient." *The Official Handbook of the Marvel Universe Deluxe Edition* #17 (August 1987). New York: Marvel Comics.

65   "living stupidly": Brown, Eliot R. "Mark Gruenwald Remembered—Part 8." www.eliotbrown.com. Circa 2017. https://www.eliotrbrown.com/wp/mark-gruenwald-remembered-part-viii/. Accessed July 30, 2021.

65   "editorial package": Gruenwald, Mark. "Changing Frequencies" (editorial). *Official Handbook of the Marvel Universe Deluxe Edition* #14 (January 1987).

65   "become outdated": "Marvel Age Interview Special." *Marvel Age* #24 (March 1985). New York: Marvel Comics.

66   "terminal burn-out": Gruenwald, Mark. "Changing Frequencies." *The Official Handbook of the Marvel Universe Deluxe Edition* #14 (January 1987). New York: Marvel Comics.

66   "pathetic look": Wright, Gregory. "From the Doghouse." *The Official Handbook of the Marvel Universe Update '89* (July 1989). New York: Marvel Comics.

66   "start all over": Gruenwald, Mark. Editorial. *The Official Handbook of the Marvel Universe Master Edition* #7 (June 1991). New York: Marvel Comics.

67   "lighthouse lamp": Brown, Eliot R. "Mark Gruenwald Remembered!—Part 4." www.eliotbrown.com. Circa 2017. https://www.eliotrbrown.com/wp/mark-gruenwald-remember-part-4/. Accessed July 30, 2021.

CHAPTER 7. SQUADRON SUPREME (1985-1989)

68   "greater variety": Bergin, Mary. "'Augmento' creator edits comics." *The Oshkosh Northwestern*. October 27, 1979.

69   "consistent ones": "Captain America." *Amazing Heroes Preview Special* #1 (Summer 1985).

69   "welcome respite": Joplin, Maralan. "Squadron Supreme." *Telegraph Wire* #24 (1985) (Comics & Comix CA store giveaway).

71   "foreign invaders": DeMatteis, J. M., and Don Perlin. *Defenders* #112 (October 1982). New York: Marvel Comics.

71   "death itself": Gruenwald, Mark, and Bob Hall. *Squadron Supreme* #1 (September 1985). New York: Marvel Comics.

71   "force them": Gruenwald, Mark, and Bob Hall. *Squadron Supreme* #1 (September 1985). New York: Marvel Comics.

72	"at least expedient": Smay, David. "Interview: Mark Gruenwald." *Amazing Heroes* #97 (June 15, 1986).
72	"real Mark Gruenwald": Macchio, Ralph. "The Road to Utopia." *Squadron Supreme*. 1997. New York: Marvel Comics.
72	"create it": Gruenwald, Mark, and Paul Ryan. *Squadron Supreme* #12 (August 1986). New York: Marvel Comics.
73	"selfsame entities": Macchio, Ralph. "The Road to Utopia." *Squadron Supreme*. 1997. New York: Marvel Comics.
74	"going to do": Smay, David. "Interview: Mark Gruenwald." *Amazing Heroes* #97 (June 15, 1986).
75	"traditional comic booking": Fiffe, Michael. "Overword 4: Squadron Supreme & Quasar." *The Comics Journal* (Fiffe Files). May 7, 2019. http://www.tcj.com/overword-4-%C2%B7-squadron-supreme-quasar/.
75	"mainstream comics": Roberson, Chris. Monday, July 2, 2007. "Mark Gruenwald, the father of modern superhero comics." The Myriad Worlds of Chris Roberson. http://www.chrisroberson.net/2007/07/mark-gruenwald-father-of-modern.html.

CHAPTER 8. *D.P.7* AND THE NEW UNIVERSE (1986-1989)

77	"with reality": Gruenwald, Mark. Letter to the editor. *Sub-Mariner* #41 (September 1971). New York: Marvel Comics.
77	"stupidities": Johnson, Dan. "Sparks in a Bottle: The Saga of the New Universe." *Back Issue* #34 (June 2009). TwoMorrows Publishing.
79	"everywhere I could": Smay, David. "Interview: Mark Gruenwald." *Amazing Heroes* #97 (June 15, 1986).
79	"not superheroes": Gruenwald, Mark. "Mark's Remarks." *Marvel Age* #77 (August 1989). New York: Marvel Comics.
80	"relentlessly realistic": Zimmerman, Dwight Jon. "Mark Gruenwald." *David Anthony Kraft's Comics Interview* #54 (March 1988).
80	"what I want": Schmitz, Barbara A. "Man's love of art, writing leads to comic book career." *The Oshkosh Northwestern*. August 17, 1986.
81	"my job easy": Zimmerman, Dwight Jon. "Mark Gruenwald." *David Anthony Kraft's Comics Interview* #54 (March 1988).
81	"over-plotted stories": "Pro File on Paul Ryan." *D.P.7* #15 (January 1988). New York: Marvel Comics.
81	"part of me": Lee, John. "Comic Powers." *The Post-Crescent*. October 19, 1986.
81	"to the series": Johnson, Dan. "Sparks in a Bottle: The Saga of the New Universe." *Back Issue* #34 (June 2009). TwoMorrows Publishing.
83	"our characters": Johnson, Dan. "Sparks in a Bottle: The Saga of the New Universe." *Back Issue* #34 (June 2009). TwoMorrows Publishing.

83	"very normal place": Lee, John. "Comic Powers." *The Post-Crescent* (Appleton, WI). October 19, 1986.
85	"too much": Gruenwald, Mark. "Mark's Remarks." *Marvel Age* #77 (August 1989). New York: Marvel Comics.
86	"whopping good yarns": Gruenwald, Mark. "Mark's Remarks." *Marvel Age* #127 (August 1993). New York: Marvel Comics.

CHAPTER 9. CAPTAIN AMERICA (1985-1995)

87	"worthy of that trust": Gruenwald, Mark. *Captain America* #306 (June 1985). New York: Marvel Comics.
88	"Of the '80s": Gruenwald, Mark. "Mark's Remarks." *Marvel Age* #120 (January 1993). New York: Marvel Comics.
88	"fullest potential": Gruenwald, Mark. "Changing of the Guard." *Captain America* #306 (June 1985).
89	"entire country": Herdling, Glenn. "Captain America." *Marvel Age* #57 (December 1987). New York: Marvel Comics.
89	"taking seriously": "Captain America." *Amazing Heroes Preview Special* #1 (Summer 1985).
91	"hate mail": Zimmerman, Dwight Jon. "Mark Gruenwald." *David Anthony Kraft's Comics Interview* #54 (March 1988).
93	"attire and flourishes": Olsen, Jason. *Mark Gruenwald and the Star Spangled Symbolism of Captain America, 1985–1995*. Jefferson, NC: McFarland. 2021.
94	"more idealistic": Gruenwald, Mark. "Mark's Remarks. *Marvel Age* #84 (January 1990). New York: Marvel Comics.

CHAPTER 10. MARK THE EXECUTIVE EDITOR (1987-1993)

95	"it's a rocketpack":—Mark Gruenwald, *Marvel Age* #108 (January 1992). New York: Marvel Comics.
95	"mean one": Mullaney, Dean. Interview with Paul V. Allen, July 19, 2022.
95	"human being": Potts, Carl. "Marvelous Tales: Remembering Mark Gruenwald and Our Trip to Skywalker Ranch." General Electric (blog). August 2, 2010.
96	"commission or omission": Gruenwald, Mark. "Mark's Remarks." *Marvel Age* #127 (August 1993). New York: Marvel Comics.
96	"create a character": Gruenwald, Mark. "Mark's Remarks." *Marvel Age* #108 (January 1992). New York: Marvel Comics.
96	"story values": Gruenwald, Mark. "Mark's Remarks." *Iron Man* #217 (April 1987). New York: Marvel Comics.
97	"entertainment experience": Gruenwald, Mark. "Mark's Remarks." *Marvel Age* #127 (August 1993). New York: Marvel Comics.

97	"make sense": Gruenwald, Mark. "Mark's Remarks." *Marvel Age* #112 (May 1992). New York: Marvel Comics.
97	"wholesale implosion": Gruenwald, Mark. "Mark's Remarks." *Marvel Age* #112 (May 1992). New York: Marvel Comics.
97	"avant garde exhibitionist": Gruenwald, Mark. "Mark's Remarks." *Marvel Age* #99 (April 1991). New York: Marvel Comics.
98	"all-time high": Gruenwald, Mark. "Mark's Remarks." *Marvel Age* #99 (April 1991). New York: Marvel Comics.
98	"eyeteeth": Zimmerman, Dwight Jon. "Mark Gruenwald." *David Anthony Kraft's Comics Interview* #54 (March 1988).
98	"a lot of it": Zimmerman, Dwight Jon. "Mark Gruenwald." *David Anthony Kraft's Comics Interview* #54 (March 1988).
99	"know and like": Gruenwald, Mark. "Mark's Remarks." *Solo Avengers* #6 (May 1988). New York: Marvel Comics.
99	"constitutes professional quality": Gruenwald, Mark. "Mark's Remarks." *Marvel Age* #111 (April 1992). New York: Marvel Comics.
99	"in their paths": Gruenwald, Mark. "Mark's Remarks." *Marvel Age* #105 (October 1991). New York: Marvel Comics.
101	"Pointer Sisters": Gruenwald, Mark. "Mark's Remarks." *Marvel Age* #109 (February 1992). New York: Marvel Comics.
101	"turning on a light": Roy Hoglund to Paul V. Allen, December 1, 2021.

CHAPTER 11. QUASAR (1989-1994)

103	"mid-to-low popularity": Gruenwald. Mark. "Mark's Remarks." *Marvel Age* #130 (November 1993). New York: Marvel Comics.
107	"feeling lifeforms": Gruenwald, Mark and Greg Capullo. *Quasar* #21 (April 1991). New York: Marvel Comics.
108	"all others": Gruenwald, Mark. "Mark's Remarks." *Marvel Age* #123 (April 1993). New York: Marvel Comics.
108	"belief in god": "What We Do." American Humanist Association. https://americanhumanist.org/what-we-do/. Retrieved June 20, 2022.
112	"lukewarm reception": Fiffe, Michael. "Overword 4: Squadron Supreme & Quasar." *The Comics Journal* (Fiffe Files). May 7, 2019. http://www.tcj.com/overword-4-%C2%B7-squadron-supreme-quasar/.
112	"lame-o": "Hunk & Babe of the Month." *Wizard* #32 (April 1994).
112	"one-shot characters": Duke, Patrick C. Letter to the editor. *Quasar* #45 (April 1993). New York: Marvel Comics.
112	"Could I do": Gruenwald, Mark, and John Heebink. *Quasar* #60 (July 1994). New York: Marvel Comics.

CHAPTER 12. DEATH AND AFTERDEATH (1995-PRESENT)

113 "significant life": Gruenwald, Mark, to David Lofvers. April 28, 1989.
113 "you're off": Ringenberg, Steve. "Interview with Mark Gruenwald." Undated (circa 1995). Comic Art and Graffix Gallery. https://comic-art.com/interviews/gruenwal.htm.
115 "I've ever heard": Grand, Alex, and Jim Thompson. "Tom DeFalco Interview, Consummate Professional." *Comic Book Historians: An Online Fanzine.* October 21, 2019. https://comicbookhistorians.com/tom-defalco-consummate-professional/.
115 "state-of-the-art packaging": Gruenwald, Mark. Bullpen Bulletins (June/July 1995). New York: Marvel Comics.
115 "cheer people up": Schuller, Catherine. "Gru the Influencer: Leaving an Indelible Mark." *Back Issue* #103 (April 2018). TwoMorrows Publishing.
116 "career at Marvel": Gruenwald, Mark. *The Gruenwald 1995 Holiday Newsletter.* Volume 3, number 1. Alternity Enterprises.
117 "ought to know": Gruenwald, Mark. Bullpen Bulletins (July 1995). New York: Marvel Comics.
117 "find another hobby": Gruenwald, Mark. "Mark's Remarks." *Avengers* #286 (December 1987). New York: Marvel Comics.
117 "so completely engaged": Gruenwald, Mark. "Afterword." *DC vs. Marvel Comics.* New York: Marvel Comics. 1996.
120 "and should be": Howe, Sean. *Marvel Comics: The Untold Story.* New York: Harper. 2012.
120 "been among us": "Re-Mark: The Comics Industry Remembers Mark Gruenwald." *Fantastic Four* #2 (December 1996). New York: Marvel Comics.
120 "writing and editing": O'Neill, Patrick Daniel. "Marvel Editor Mark Gruenwald Dies." *Wizard* #63 (November 1996).
120 "to his work": O'Neill, Patrick Daniel. "Marvel Editor Mark Gruenwald Dies." *Wizard* #63 (November 1996).
121 "pity himself": O'Neil, Denny. "In Memoriam: Mark Gruenwald (1953–1996)." *Wizard, the Comics Magazine* #65 (January 1997).
124 "little extra lift": Gruenwald, Norma, to Susan and David Lofvers. December 22, 1977.
125 "fight another day": Gruenwald, Mark. "Bullpen Bulletins" (September 1993). New York: Marvel Comics.
126 "100 percent": Harrold, Jess. "Making a Mark on Cap." *Captain America 75th Anniversary Magazine* (June 2018). New York: Marvel Comics.

REFERENCES

CHAPTER 1. ORIGIN (1953-1971)

Coughanor, Gayle. Interview with Paul V. Allen. November 18, 2021.
Domer, Randy R. Interview with Paul V. Allen. September 25, 2021.
"Foreign Language Week Is Planned." *The Oshkosh Northwestern*. March 25, 1971.
Gruenwald, Mark. "Mark's Remarks." *Iron Man* #210 (September 1986). New York: Marvel Comics.
Gruenwald, Mark. "Mark's Remarks." *West Coast Avengers* #24 (September 1987). New York: Marvel Comics.
Haefer, Todd. "Artist Given a Marvelous Memorial." *The Oshkosh Northwestern*. May 23, 1997.
"High School Newspaper Contest Announces Area Youth Winners." *The Oshkosh Northwestern*. April 23, 1969.
"Honors, Awards Presented." *The Oshkosh Northwestern*. June 3, 1970.
"Humanities Conference Set." *The Oshkosh Northwestern*. October 9, 1971.
Lindsay, Holly. Interview with Paul V. Allen. December 5, 2021.
"Mook Takes First Place in Writing Test." *The Oshkosh Northwestern*. May 6, 1969.
"OHS Play Rates Highest Ranking." *The Oshkosh Northwestern*. November 23, 1970.
"OHS Scholarship Winners Named." *The Oshkosh Northwestern*. June 8, 1971.
"Problems, Progress Theme Of Student Grad Speeches." *The Oshkosh Northwestern*. June 9, 1971.
"Record Number to Receive OHS Diplomas." *The Oshkosh Northwestern*. June 7, 1971.
"Rock Opera by Students to Be Shown." *The Oshkosh Northwestern*. March 3, 1972.
"Teen-agers to Take Part in Pilot Summer Symposium." *The Oshkosh Northwestern*. May 19, 1969.
"Tipler Jr. High Distributes Own New Publication." *The Oshkosh Northwestern*. November 1, 1967.
"Underclassmen Get Awards." *The Oshkosh Northwestern*. June 3, 1969.
"Week's Activities in Oshkosh Churches." *The Oshkosh Northwestern*. February 14, 1970.

CHAPTER 2. COLLEGE YEARS (1972–1976)

"Augmento creators reveal everything." *Advance-Titan*. December 12, 1974.
"Augmento . . . in the beginning." *Advance-Titan*. September 5, 1975.
Bock, Edith. "Radio drama lives!" *The Post-Crescent*. April 20, 1975.
DeShaney, Ginger. "It's a bird, it's a plane—it's Super Mark." *The Oshkosh Northwestern*. October 24, 1989.
Gruenwald, Mark. "Fanzy Colors." *Personal Entropy* #1 (December 1976). Alternity Enterprises.
Gruenwald, Mark. "Mark's Remarks." *Solo Avengers* #2 (January 1988). New York: Marvel Comics.
Leubke, Debbie. "'Peter and the Wolf' is delightful musical." *The Oshkosh Northwestern*. February 18, 1974.
Lofvers, David. E-mail to Paul V. Allen. May 4, 2022.
Lofvers, David. E-mail to Paul V. Allen. May 10, 2022.
"Tryouts Are Scheduled for Production of 'Hello Dolly.'" *The Oshkosh Northwestern*. February 18, 1974.

CHAPTER 3. INTO THE OMNIVERSE (1976–1978)

"Arnold Jules Glass." *Chicago Tribune*. April 12, 2020. https://www.legacy.com/us/obituaries/chicagotribune/name/arnold-glass-obituary?id=2818907.
Bergin, Mary. "'Augmento' creator edits comics." *The Oshkosh Northwestern*. October 27, 1979.
Brown, Eliot R. "Mark Gruenwald Remembered Some More—Part 3." www.eliotbrown.com. Circa 2017. https://www.eliotrbrown.com/wp/mark-gruenwald-remembered-some-more-part-three/. Accessed July 30, 2021.
"Father, son combine." *The Oshkosh Northwestern*. July 28, 1977.
Gerds, Warren. "East High graduate acts in operas." *Green Bay Press-Gazette*. February 13, 1983.
"Glass, Gruenwald." *The Oshkosh Northwestern*. July 6, 1981.
Gruenwald, Mark, to David Lofvers. March 6, 1977.
Gruenwald, Myron. *A Primer on Reality in Comic Books*. 1977. Alternity Enterprises.
"It's the Real Thing!: A Review of Mark Gruenwald's 'A Treatise of Reality in Comic Literature.'" Kim Thompson. *Woweekazowie* #2 (Fall 1976).
Jeffrey, Scott. *The Posthuman Body in Superhero Comics: Superhuman, Transhuman, Post/Human*. New York: Palgrave. 2016.
Murdough, Adam C. "Worlds Will Live, Worlds Will Die: Myth, Metatext, Continuity and Cataclysm in DC Comics' Crisis on Infinite Earths." Dissertation. Bowling Green State University. 2006. https://etd.ohiolink.edu/.
Shooter, Jim. "Writer/Editors, Part 2." August 11, 2011. Jim Shooter.com. http://jimshooter.com/2011/08/writereditors-part-2.html/.

Shooter, Jim. "Writer/Editors, Part 4." August 17, 2011. Jim Shooter.com. http://jimshooter.com/2011/08/writereditors-part-4.html/.
Zimmerman, Dwight Jon. "Denny O'Neil." *David Anthony Kraft's Comics Interview* #35 (August 1986).
Zimmerman, Dwight Jon. "The Marvel Age Interview: Mark Gruenwald." *Marvel Age* #56 (November 1987).

CHAPTER 4. WRITER AND ARTIST (1978-1984)

Brevoort, Tom. "Five More Times Marvel Referenced DC Characters in Interesting Ways." February 6, 2021. Tombrevoort.com. https://tombrevoort.com/2021/02/06/5bc-five-more-times-marvel-referenced-dc-characters-in-interesting-ways/.
Buttery, Jerrold. "What If?: Infinite Alternate Realities." *Back Issue* #111 (April 2019). TwoMorrows Publishing.
Gruenwald, Mark. "Sometimes the Good Guys Lose." *Marvel Age* #2 (May 1983). New York: Marvel Comics.

CHAPTER 5. MARK THE EDITOR (1982-1987)

Brown, Eliot R. "Spider-Woman #50—The Most Expensive Comic Cover Ever Made! Part 2." Eliot R. Brown.com. https://www.eliotrbrown.com/wp/spider-woman-50-the-most-expensive-comic-cover-ever-made-part-2/.
Busiek, Kurt, et al. "A Day in the Life of Marvel Comics." *Marvel Age* #35 (February 1986). New York: Marvel Comics.
Carlin, Mike, and Mark Gruenwald. "Grumblings from the Gru Crew." *Marvel Age* #4 (July 1983). New York: Marvel Comics.
Dallas, Keith. *American Comic Book Chronicles*, Vol.13. TwoMorrows Publishing (January 2013).
Daniels, Les. *Marvel: Five Fabulous Decades of the World's Greatest Comics*. Abrams. 1991.
Gruenwald, Mark. "Behind the Lines: What's an editor to do?" *Marvel Age* #9 (December 1983). New York: Marvel Comics.
Gruenwald, Mark. "Mark's Remarks." Avengers #269 (July 1986). New York: Marvel Comics.
Gruenwald, Mark. "Mark's Remarks." *Avengers* #278 (April 1987). New York: Marvel Comics.
Gruenwald, Mark. "Mark's Remarks." *West Coast Avengers* #25 (October 1987). New York: Marvel Comics.
Gruenwald, Mark. "Mark's Remarks." *West Coast Avengers* #27 (December 1987). New York: Marvel Comics.
Gruenwald, Mark. "Mark's Remarks." *Avengers* #287 (January 1988). New York: Marvel Comics.

Gruenwald, Mark. "Mark's Remarks." *Iron Man* #226 (January 1988). New York: Marvel Comics.

Gruenwald, Mark. "Mark's Remarks." *Avengers* #288 (February 1988). New York: Marvel Comics.

Gruenwald, Mark. "Mark's Remarks." *West Coast Avengers* #31 (April 1988). New York: Marvel Comics.

Gruenwald, Mark. "Mark's Remarks." *Marvel Age* #90 (July 1990). New York: Marvel Comics.

Gruenwald, Mark. "Mark's Remarks." *Marvel Age* #122 (March 1993). New York: Marvel Comics.

Gruenwald, Mark. "Mark's Remarks." Marvel Age #125 (June 1993). New York: Marvel Comics.

O'Connell, Aaron. Interview with Paul V. Allen. December 2, 2021.

CHAPTER 6. *THE OFFICIAL HANDBOOK OF THE MARVEL UNIVERSE* (1983-1993)

Brown, Eliot R. "Mark Gruenwald A Remembrance—Part 1." www.eliotbrown.com. Circa 2017. https://www.eliotrbrown.com/wp/mark-gruenwald-a-remembrance/. Accessed July 30, 2021.

Dallas, Keith. *American Comic Book Chronicles*, Vol. 13. TwoMorrows Publishing (January 2013).

Daniels, Les. Marvel: Five Fabulous Decades of the World's Greatest Comics. Harry N. Abrams. 1993.

Gruenwald, Mark. "Mark's Remarks." *Marvel Age* #94 (November 1990). New York: Marvel Comics.

Sanderson, Peter. "Guidebook to the Cosmos." *Marvel Age* #1 (September 1983).

"The Official Handbook of the Marvel Universe—Update." *Marvel Age* #75 (June 1989). New York: Marvel Comics.

CHAPTER 7. *SQUADRON SUPREME* (1985-1989)

Hart, Ken. "Squadron Supreme." *Marvel Age* #29 (August 1985). New York: Marvel Comics.

Lofvers, David. E-mail to Paul V. Allen. June 16, 2022.

Macchio, Ralph. "The Road to Utopia." *Squadron Supreme*. 1997. New York: Marvel Comics.

Sanderson, Peter. "When Super-Heroes Rule: The Squadron Supreme." *Amazing Heroes* #70 (May 1, 1985).

Sanderson, Peter. "Mark of Excellence." *Back Issue* #19 (November 2006). TwoMorrows Publishing.

CHAPTER 8. *D.P.7* AND THE NEW UNIVERSE (1986-1989)

Dallas, Keith. *American Comic Book Chronicles*, Vol. 13 (January 2013). TwoMorrows Publishing.

Grant, Paul J. "Urban Renewal." *Wizard, the Comics Magazine* #53 (January 1996).

Gruenwald, Mark. "Mark's Remarks." *Marvel Age* #93 (October 1990). New York: Marvel Comics.

Gruenwald, Mark. "A Memo From Mark." *Captain America* #443 (September 1994). New York: Marvel Comics.

Lofvers, David. Interview with Paul V. Allen. January 6, 2022.

Sanderson, Peter. "A Tale of Two Captains: An Interview with Mark Gruenwald on Captain America." *Amazing Heroes* #146 (August 1, 1988).

Zimmerman, Dwight Jon. "Mark Gruenwald." *David Anthony Kraft's Comics Interview* #54 (March 1988).

CHAPTER 9. *CAPTAIN AMERICA* (1985-1995)

Gruenwald, Mark. "Mark's Remarks." *Marvel Age* #131 (December 1993). New York: Marvel Comics.

Wheeler, Andrew. "Fabian Nicieza: Working For The Man." Popimage.com. June 2000. https://web.archive.org/web/20160303235907/http://www.popimage.com/industrial/062000nicezaint.html.

CHAPTER 10. MARK THE EXECUTIVE EDITOR (1987-1993)

Brevoort, Tom. "Blah Blah Blog—Mark Gruenwald Memorial." April 28, 2007. Tom Brevoort.com. https://tombrevoort.com/2020/05/24/blah-blah-blog-mark-gruenwald-memorial/.

Brown, Eliot R. "Mark Gruenwald Remembered—Part 8." www.eliotbrown.com. Circa 2017. https://www.eliotrbrown.com/wp/mark-gruenwald-remembered-part-viii/. Accessed July 30, 2021.

Denee, Marie. "Up close and personal with Catherine Schuller." The Curvy Fashionista. Date unknown. https://thecurvyfashionista.com/up-close-and-personal-with-catherine-schuller/.

Gruenwald, Mark. "Mark's Remarks." *Solo Avengers* #7 (June 1988). New York: Marvel Comics.

Gruenwald, Mark. Bullpen Bulletins (May 1989). New York: Marvel Comics.

Gruenwald, Mark. "Mark's Remarks." *Marvel Age* #74 (May 1989). New York: Marvel Comics.

Gruenwald, Mark. "Mark's Remarks." *Marvel Age* #91 (August 1990). New York: Marvel Comics.

Gruenwald, Mark. "Mark's Remarks." *Marvel Age* #98 (March 1991). New York: Marvel Comics.

Gruenwald, Mark. "Mark's Remarks." *Marvel Age* #117 (October 1992). New York: Marvel Comics.

Gruenwald, Mark. "Mark's Remarks." *Marvel Age* #119 (December 1992). New York: Marvel Comics.

Gruenwald, Mark. Bullpen Bulletins (September 1993). New York: Marvel Comics.

Gruenwald, Mark. Bullpen Bulletins (December 1993). New York: Marvel Comics.

Gruenwald, Mark. Bullpen Bulletins (July 1994). New York: Marvel Comics.

"I Am Rose—Catherine Schuller." See Rose Go. Undated.https://seerosego.com/blogs/seerosego/i-am-rose-catherine-schuller.

Jones, LaMont. "Schuller wrote the book on plus-size modeling." *Pittsburgh Post-Gazette*. October 19, 2003.

Last, Jonathan V. "The Crash of 1993." *Washington Examiner*. June 13, 2011. https://www.washingtonexaminer.com/weekly-standard/the-crash-of-1993.

Sanderson, Peter. "When Super-Heroes Rule: The Squadron Supreme." *Amazing Heroes* #70 (May 1, 1985).

Schmitz, Barbara A. "Man's love of art, writing leads to comic book career." *The Oshkosh Northwestern*. August 17, 1986.

Schuller, Catherine. "Gru the Influencer: Leaving an Indelible Mark." *Back Issue* #103 (April 2018). TwoMorrows Publishing.

Young, Bud. "No-Prize Podcast Special: Catherine Schuller & Sara Gruenwald." No-Prize Podcast. October 28, 2021. https://undercovercapes.com/no-prize-podcast-special-catherine-schuller-sara-gruenwald/.

CHAPTER 11. *QUASAR* (1989-1994)

Ashford, Richard. "The Man Who Runs the Universe." *Speakeasy* #98 (May 1989).

DeRoss, Jennifer. Forgotten All-Star: A Biography of Gardner Fox. Pulp Hero Press. 2019.

Gruenwald, Mark. "Book Explains 'Black Arts.'" *The Oshkosh Northwestern*. June 27, 1969.

Gruenwald, Mark. "Mark's Remarks." *Marvel Age* #90 (July 1990). New York: Marvel Comics.

Gruenwald, Mark. "Mark's Remarks." *Marvel Age* #123 (April 1993). New York: Marvel Comics.

Gruenwald, Mark. "Mark's Remarks." *Marvel Age* #131 (December 1993). New York: Marvel Comics.

Gruenwald, Mark. "Last Will and Testament of Mark Gruenwald." Executed May 22, 1993.

Lofvers, David to Paul V. Allen. June 12, 2022.

Sanderson, Peter. "The Coming of Quasar." *Marvel Age* #78 (September 1989).

Smay, David. "Interview: Mark Gruenwald." *Amazing Heroes* #97 (June 15, 1986).

CHAPTER 12. DEATH AND AFTERDEATH (1995–PRESENT)

Brevoort, Tom. "Blah Blah Blog—Mark Gruenwald Memorial." April 28, 2007. Tom Brevoort.com. https://tombrevoort.com/2020/05/24/blah-blah-blog-mark-gruenwald-memorial/.

Brown, Eliot R. "Mark Gruenwald Reconsidered—He Liked Music, Did He Ever—Part 6." www.eliotbrown.com. Circa 2017. https://www.eliotrbrown.com/wp/mark-gruenwald-reconsidered-part-vi-he-liked-music-did-he-ever/. Accessed 30 July 30, 2021.

Catto, Ed. "The Mark Gruenwald Tribute." ComicMix. July 4, 2016. https://www.comicmix.com/2016/07/04/ed-catto-the-mark-gruenwald-tribute/.

Cornell, Paul. "The Twelve Blogs of Christmas: Seven. Omniverse #1." December 19, 2021. https://www.paulcornell.com/2021/12/the-12-blogs-of-christmas-seven-omniverse-1/.

David, Peter. "Grueneycon." *Comics Buyers' Guide* #1194 (October 4, 1996). Republished February 2, 2012, at Peter David.net.

De Blieck Jr., Augie. "The Commentary Track: Spider-Man Family 'Ringo Tribute.'" Comic Book Resources. February 22, 2008. https://web.archive.org/web/20080225150848/www.comicbookresources.com/news/newsitem.cgi?id=13091.

Gruenwald, Cat Schuller. "CosMODA: The Cosplay Runway." Fashion Week Online. Undated. https://fashionweekonline.com/cosmoda-the-cosplay-runway. Retrieved Accessed July 1, 2022.

Gruenwald, Cat Schuller. "Mark Gruenwald, His Ashes and Me." 13th Dimension. August 12, 2016. https://13thdimension.com/mark-gruenwald-his-ashes-and-me/.

Haefer, Todd. "Artist enshrined." *The Oshkosh Northwestern*. June 17, 1997.

Haefer, Todd. "Comic's gifts remembered." *The Oshkosh Northwestern*. October 13, 1996.

Haefer, Todd. "Editors, Friends recall Gruenwald's creativity, humor." *The Oshkosh Northwestern*. 15 August 15, 1996.

Lovett, Jamie. "Captain America's Shield Is Part Of Stephen Colbert's Late Show Set." Comicbook.com. September 6, 2017. https://comicbook.com/news/captain-americas-shield-is-part-of-stephen-colberts-late-show-se/.

"Mark E. Gruenwald, writer of comics." *Poughkeepsie Journal*. August 13, 1996.

"Mark E. Gruenwald." *The Oshkosh Northwestern*. August 13, 1996.

Napier, Claire. "Bob Harras: An Oral History in Collage." February 12, 2021. Women Write About Comics. https://womenwriteaboutcomics.com/2021/02/bob-harras-an-oral-history-in-collage/.

Neary, Paul. Bullpen Bulletins.—June 1993 (*Fantastic Four* #377 (June 1993). Paul Neary.

Perry, Tom. "Comic Book Challenge honors Oshkosh native, comic book legend." *The Oshkosh Northwestern*. 3 June 3, 2019.

Reyes, Amy. "Comic-book writer's ashes mixed with ink of Marvel special edition." *The Anniston Star*. September 1, 1997.

Salicrup, Jim. "A Few Words About Mark Gruenwald." *MoCCAZine: The Newsletter for the Museum of Comic and Cartoon Art.* September/October 2006.

Schuller, Catherine. "Gru the Influencer: Leaving an Indelible Mark." *Back Issue* #103 (April 2018).

Tipton, Scott. "Gone Too Soon: Remembering Da Gru." Comics 101. A Site Called Fred./ September 15, 2004. https://web.archive.org/web/20110723181802/http://asitecalledfred.com/comics101/82.html.

Van Lente, Fred. "The Top 13 Roger Stern Avengers Stories—Ranked." 13th Dimension. September 17, 2020. https://13thdimension.com/the-top-13-roger-stern-avengers-stories-ranked/.

INDEX

Adams, Neal, 18, 22, 26
Advance-Titan, 16–18
Alternity Enterprises, 31, 41, 61, 106
Amalgam Comics, 117
Amazing World of DC Comics, 32, 33, 37
Aquarian, The, 39, 71, 108
Archer, Jane, 11, 12
Augmento, 15, 17–20, 26, 107
Avengers, The, 9, 34, 41, 43, 47, 49–53, 58, 63, 68, 104, 115, 121, 126

Backus, Jerry, 13
Bails, Jerry, 23, 31
Batman, 8, 37, 68, 71, 117
Battlestar, 91, 126
Berkenwald, Martin, 27, 34
Bizarre Adventures, 44, 45
Black Goliath, 39, 40
Brown, Cecelia, 16
Brown, Eliot R., 47, 54, 55, 57, 58, 60, 62, 63, 65, 67
Bukowski, Bill, 17, 18
Bulandi, Danny, 81, 82, 94, 104
Buscema, John, 50, 68, 75
Buscema, Sal, 68
Byrne, John, 39, 40, 42, 57, 62, 84

CAPA-Alpha, 31
Captain America: "The Captain," 90–92; DeMatteis's removal from title, 59; Gruenwald's removal from title, 113; morality, 88–91; patriotism, 87, 88; political views, 88, 89; relevance, 93, 94; villains, 89, 90
Capullo, Greg, 106, 109, 110
Carlin, Mike, 49, 55, 57, 59, 62, 117, 120, 121
Casper the Friendly Ghost, 6, 107
Celestials, 40, 42
Cheap Laffs, 55, 57, 97, 121
Codename: Spitfire, 78, 83, 84
Combo Man, 116
Comic Buyer's Guide, 23, 112
Complete Justice League of America Reader, The, 23, 24, 29, 32, 60
Concept, 12, 16
Concept Radio Theatre, 16, 17, 108
Contest of Champions, 44, 61, 62, 123
Coughanour, Gayle, 6–10, 105, 106, 118, 129
Crossbones, 93, 114
Crystar, 44

Daredevil, 21, 37
David, Peter, 54, 84, 121
DeFalco, Tom, 37, 51, 54, 59, 77, 85, 95, 98, 114, 115, 121
DeMatteis, J. M., 50, 58, 59, 71
Diamondback, 92, 114
Dillin, Dick, 26
Ditko, Steve, 31, 37, 49, 64
Domer, Randy, 8

D.P.7: autobiographical elements, 81, 83; characters, 79; creation, 79; return in *Quasar*, 109; storytelling approach, 79–81

Eclipse Comics, 31
Englehart, Steve, 68, 71, 87
Eon, 104, 107
Epoch, 107
Eternals, The, 42, 104, 105, 109, 110

Fantastic Four, 9, 12, 36, 43, 96, 115, 116, 126
Flag-Smasher, 89, 90, 126
Flash, The, 8, 30, 68, 105
Fiffe, Michael, 74, 75, 112
Fox, Gardner, 22, 29, 31, 33, 69, 105
Frenz, Ron, 59
Friedrich, Mike, 23

Galton, James, 77
Gerber, Steve, 36
G.I. Joe: A Real American Hero, 88, 89
Giant Man, 39, 40
Gibbons, Dave, 74
Gillis, Peter B., 62
Glass, Belinda, 44, 46, 55, 58, 100, 129
Goodwin, Archie, 32, 34, 36, 38, 77
Grant, Steven, 40, 42, 44, 47, 57, 126
Green Lantern, 8, 37, 68, 105
Greenbaum, Jan, 101
Gruenwald, Gayle, 6–10, 105, 106, 118, 129
Gruenwald, Mark: as artist, 3, 7, 10, 12, 13, 15–20, 24–26, 33, 45–48, 65; continuity philosophy, 32, 34, 35, 64, 75, 86, 96, 97, 126; death, 118, 119; education, 10–17; political views, 88, 89; religious views, 107, 108; time travel philosophy, 19, 34, 43, 96, 126

Gruenwald, Myron, 3, 6, 8–10, 21, 76, 88, 124, 129
Gruenwald, Norma, 3, 5, 8, 10, 18, 21, 107, 124, 129
Gruenwald, Sara, 58, 99, 100–102, 118, 125, 126, 129
Gypsy Moth, 38, 55

Haasl, Charlie, 13, 15, 17, 83
Hall, Bob, 51, 68, 70, 75
Hama, Larry, 57, 102
Harvey Comics, 6, 107
Hawkeye, 46–48, 63, 64, 104, 114
Heebink, John, 110–12
Her, 108
Hoglund, Roy "Chuck," 3, 11, 13, 15–18, 20, 28, 83, 101, 124
Hulk, The, 44, 47, 48, 50
Hyperion, 68, 71, 72, 74, 109

Icarus, 13, 15, 16, 18
Infantino, Carmine, 26, 38
Iron Man, 49, 50, 52, 53, 59, 63

Julycon, 22. See also New York Comic Art Convention
Justice, 78, 84
Justice League of America (JLA), 6–9, 21, 25, 26, 31, 37, 68, 69, 83, 105. See also *Complete Justice League of America Reader, The*
Justice Society of America, 16, 23, 29, 74

Kane, Gil, 18, 34
Kickers, Inc., 78, 83–85
Kirby, Jack, 22, 37, 42, 49–51, 60, 64, 104
Kitchen, Denis, 17
Kismet, 108

Lee, Stan, 12, 38, 49, 53, 54, 64, 73, 87, 120
Levitz, Paul, 32, 121

Lim, Ron, 93, 94
Lindsay, Holly, 12, 13, 15, 44, 81, 106
Lofvers, David, 22–24, 29, 45, 46, 57, 81, 119, 121, 123

Macalester College, 15, 44
Macchio, Ralph, 32, 36, 39, 53, 59, 72, 73, 97, 101, 103, 126
Mackie, Howard, 57, 83, 84, 104
Madison, J. Mark, 10, 12, 13, 20, 83
Maelstrom, 108, 109
Magneto, 42
Mantlo, Bill, 43, 44
"Mark's Remarks," 53, 58, 85, 93, 96, 98, 117, 125, 129
Martian Manhunter, 32
Marvel Age, 59, 65, 98, 108, 109
Marvel Cinematic Universe, 126
Marvel Team-Up, 37, 47, 96, 103, 104
Marvel Two-In-One, 39, 40, 46, 103
Marvelution, 114–16
Maximoff, Wanda, 40, 41, 126
McDuffie, Dwayne, 91
Michelinie, David, 42, 50
Mighty Thor, The, 40, 43, 46, 50, 51
Mobius, Mobius M., 126, 128
Mockingbird, 47, 96
Monty Python's Flying Circus, 55, 59, 122
Morelli, Jack, 57, 79
Mullaney, Dean, 31, 41, 60

Needle, The, 38
New Universe: cancellation, 85; continuation, 109; guiding principles, 77, 78; origin, 77, 78; *The Pitt*, 84; sales, 83, 85; titles, 78
New York Comic Art Convention, 21, 29, 31, 33
Nighthawk, 68, 71–73
Nightmask, 78, 83, 84

O'Connell, Wendell, 106
O'Neil, Dennis, 21, 23, 32, 37, 50–52, 54, 120, 121
Official Handbook of the Marvel Universe (OHOTMU): creators, 63; legacy, 67; precursors, 61, 62; successive editions, 65–67
Omniverse, 33–35, 41, 62, 96, 121
"Operation Galactic Storm," 93, 110
Oshkosh, Wisconsin, 5, 6, 9–11, 105, 106, 121, 124, 125
Outer Limits, The, 10

Pawling, New York, 100, 118, 119
"Pegasus Project, The," 39, 40, 71, 76, 103
Perez, George, 39, 40, 68
Personal Entropy, 31, 107
Pollard, Keith, 40, 43, 61, 66
Poplaski, Pete, 17, 34, 35, 59

Quasar: artists, 100; autobiographical elements, 105–7; cancellation, 110; character origin, 103, 104; connections to previous work, 108–10; death as a theme, 107; early appearances, 103, 104; failure as a theme, 110, 112; religion as a theme, 108
Questprobe, 48, 110
Quicksilver, 41, 42

Reagan, Ronald, 78, 88, 91
Red Skull, 92, 93
Roberson, Chris, 75
Ryan, Paul, 68, 75, 76, 81–83, 104, 110

Salicrup, Jim, 36, 39
San Diego Comic Con, 97, 122, 127
Sanderson, Peter, 62, 66
Scarlet Witch, 40, 41, 126
Schuller, Catherine, 101, 102, 120–25, 127, 129

Schwartz, Julius "Julie," 25, 26, 32, 37, 69
Sekowsky, Mike, 21
Serpent Society, 89, 92, 124
Seuling, Phil, 21
Shooter, Jim, 34–37, 46, 50–52, 58, 61, 62, 77, 78, 83, 95
Shroud, The, 69, 71
Simonson, Walt, 51, 62, 120, 121, 126
Son of Santa, 45
Spectrum, 11, 12
Spider-Man, 9, 28, 29, 31, 44, 47, 50, 59, 61, 73, 103, 116
Spider-Woman (Jessica Drew), 37–39, 42, 46, 47, 55, 56, 61, 71, 116
Squadron Supreme: comparison to *Watchmen*, 74, 75; early appearances, 68, 71; legacy, 75, 76; later appearances, 76, 108, 109, 116; similarities to Justice League of America, 68, 69
Star Brand, 78, 84, 109
Starblast, 110, 116
Stern, Roger, 34, 50–53, 61
Strange, Adam, 16, 105
Superman, 6, 8, 10, 21, 29, 68, 117

Terpsichore, 16, 20, 81
Thomas, Roy, 23, 36, 40, 49, 68
Three Stooges, The, 54, 81, 129
Threshold, 16
Time Variance Authority, 126
Treatise on Reality in Comic Literature, A (TORICL), 28–31, 33, 43, 96
Truesdale, Dave, 25
Twilight Zone, The, 10, 16, 107, 121, 122

University of Wisconsin–Oshkosh, 9, 14, 17, 90, 106, 124
US Agent, 90–92, 114, 126

Vaughan, Wendell. *See* Quasar
Veidemanis, Gladys, 13

Walker, John, 90–92, 114, 126
Watchmen, 74
Waverly, Iowa, 5, 64
Wein, Len, 36, 58
West Coast Avengers, 50, 53, 59, 92
What If . . . , 31, 34, 36, 37, 42, 47, 119
Who's Who: The Definitive Directory to the DC Universe, 65
Wilburn, John, 27, 28, 44
Wilson, Ron, 40, 42, 126
Wizard Magazine, 112, 120
Wolfman, Marv, 36, 38, 43
Wonder Woman, 8, 16, 21
Wright, Gene, 13, 83
Wright, Gregory, 66
Wundagore, 42, 126
Wundarr, 39, 71, 108

X-Men, 9, 21, 57, 116

"Yesterday Quest," 41, 126

Zeck, Mike, 50, 58, 90

ABOUT THE AUTHOR

Photo courtesy of the author

Paul V. Allen is a nonfiction author who writes about the lives of creative people. He lives in Normal, Illinois, with his wife, two sons, two cats, and a room full of comic books.

www.ingramcontent.com/pod-product-compliance
Lightning Source LLC
Chambersburg PA
CBHW071004160426
43193CB00012B/1918